The Third Testimony

ʿAlī عليه السلام in the Adhān

Compiled and Translated by Saleem Bhimji
Edited by Arifa Hudda

The Third Testimony: ʿAlī ﷺ in the Adhān

Compiled and Translated by Saleem Bhimji
Edited by Arifa Hudda

Question & Answer provided by www.islamquest.net @
http://www.islamquest.net/fa/archive/question/fa923

First Published in 2022 by
Islamic Publishing House
www.iph.ca · iph@iph.ca

ISBN: 978-1-927930-22-9

Cover Design and Layout by Islamic Publishing House

Contents

Introduction i

Question 11

Concise Answer to this Question 11

Detailed Answer to this Question 13

A. Method of the Prophet ﷺ for the Adhān and Iqāmah ... 14

B. Testimony to the Authority of Imam ʿAlī ؑ in the Adhān, Iqāmah and Talqīn 16

C. Bearing Witness to Imam al-Zāman ؑ in the *Adhān* . 28

Appendix I 29

Innovation in the 'Sunni' Adhān 29

Fatāwā of the Major Shīʿa Scholars 31

Āyatullāh al-ʿUẓmā Shaykh Jawādī Āmulī 33
Āyatullāh al-ʿUẓmā Sayyid ʿAbdul Karīm Mūsawī Ardebilī 33
Āyatullāh al-ʿUẓmā Sayyid ʿAlavī Gurgānī 33
Āyatullāh al-ʿUẓmā Shaykh Nūrī Hamadānī 34
Āyatullāh al-ʿUẓmā Sayyid ʿAlī Ḥusaynī Khāmeneʾī 34
Āyatullāh al-ʿUẓmā Shaykh Waḥīd Khurasānī 35
Āyatullāh al-ʿUẓmā Shaykh Ḥusayn Mazāherī 35
Āyatullāh al-ʿUẓmā Sayyid Taqī Modarresī 36
Āyatullāh al-ʿUẓmā Sayyid Ṣadiq Roḥānī 36
Āyatullāh al-ʿUẓmā Sayyid ʿAlī Ḥusaynī Sīstānī 37
Āyatullāh al-ʿUẓmā Sayyid Muḥammad Ḥusaynī Shahrūdī 38
Āyatullāh al-ʿUẓmā Shaykh Nāṣir Makārim Shīrāzī 38
Āyatullāh al-ʿUẓmā Sayyid Ṣādiq Shīrāzī 39
Āyatullāh al-ʿUẓmā Shaykh Jaʿfar Subḥānī 39
Āyatullāh al-ʿUẓmā Shaykh Mujtabā Ṭehrānī 40
Āyatullāh al-ʿUẓmā Sayyid Shubayrī Zanjānī 40
Late Āyatullāh al-ʿUẓmā Muḥammad Taqī Behjat 41
Late Āyatullāh al-ʿUẓmā Sayyid Muḥammad Burujerdī 42
Late Āyatullāh al-ʿUẓmā Shaykh Luṭfullāh Ṣāfī Gulpāygānī 42
Late Āyatullāh al-ʿUẓmā Sayyid Ruḥullāh Khomeinī 43

Late Āyatullāh al-ʿUẓmā Shaykh Fādhil Lankarānī....................43
Late Āyatullāh al-ʿUẓmā Sayyid Muḥammad Shīrāzī....................43
Late Āyatullāh al-ʿUẓmā Mīrzā Jawād Tabrizī....................44

Appendix II....................45

Islamic Laws of the *Adhān* and *Iqāmah*....................45

Method of Performing the *Adhān* and *Iqāmah*....................46

Translation of the lines of the *Adhān* and *Iqāmah*....................48

Conditions Regarding the *Adhān* and *Iqāmah*....................48

Times when the Adhān is not Required....................54

Times When the Adhān and Iqāmah are Not Required....................55

Other Rulings of the *Adhān* and *Iqāmah*....................59

Recommended Actions of the *Adhān* and *Iqāmah*....................59

Appendix III....................63

Supplications to Recite While the Adhān is Being Recited....63

At the Completion of the Adhān....................65

Other Publications Available....................67

Introduction

By Shaykh Saleem Bhimji

In the tenth year after the migration to Medina, the year which later became known as *ḥajjat al-widāʿ* [The (year of the) farewell *ḥajj*], the Muslims who had accompanied the Noble Prophet ﷺ to Mecca were finishing their *ḥajj* rites – the first and last *ḥajj* which the Prophet would ever perform. Once the pilgrimage was complete, the Prophet ﷺ and those with him were making their way back to Medina and the other cities from which they had come. When they reached Rābigh – an area around five kilometers from Juḥfah, one of the *miqāt* [the spot where those performing the pilgrimage to Mecca would don the ceremonial clothing – the iḥrām] for the *ḥujjāj* - the order came from Allah to halt the entire caravan.

At this point, the truthful conveyor of the revelation, angel Jibrāʾīl ؑ came to the Prophet ﷺ who was stationed in the watering-hole valley known as *Ghadīr* and revealed the following verse of the Quran to him:

﴿يَا أَيُّهَا الرَّسُولُ بَلِّـغْ مَا أُنْزِلَ إِلَيْكَ مِنْ رَبِّكَ وَ إِنْ لَمْ تَفْعَلْ فَمَا بَلَّغْتَ رِسَالَتَهُ وَاللهُ يَعْصِمُكَ مِنَ النَّاسِ...﴾

O' Messenger! Convey that which has been revealed to you from your Lord and if you do not do so, it is as if you have not conveyed His message at all, and Allah will protect you from the people...[1]

Since this verse commanded the Prophet ﷺ to stop right where he was, he and those with him, halted in the valley of *Ghadīr*.

It was noontime and as can be expected, the weather was extremely hot. The Prophet ﷺ performed the afternoon prayers in congregation, and then with the multitudes of people around him, he ascended a small platform built from camel saddles and other things that the Muslims had with them.

In a loud voice, he gave a long speech and said to the people: O' people! Know that shortly I will answer the call of the Truth (Allah) and will no longer be among you – I have a responsibility (to Allah) and you too have a responsibility (towards Him).

The Prophet ﷺ then mentioned something very important to the people and stated:
I am leaving behind two weighty things to you as a trust – one of them is the Book of Allah, and the other is my family, the Ahlul Bayt. These two shall never separate from one another. O' people! Do not attempt to supersede the Quran or my family, and do not be negligent in your actions towards these two, because if you do so, then you will be destroyed.

After stating this, he took the hand of 'Alī ؑ, raised it up and introduced him to the multitudes of people and asked:

---

[1] Quran, Sūrah al-Mā'idah (5), verse 67.

Who has more of a right over the believers than their own selves?

Everyone present proclaimed:
Allah and His Prophet know better.

The Noble Prophet ﷺ then said:
Allah is my Master and I am the master of all of the believers, and I have more right and authority over the believers than they have over their own selves.

Then he continued:

مَنْ كُنْتُ مَوْلَاهُ فَهَذَا عَلِيٌّ مَوْلَاهُ. أَللَّهُمَّ وَالِ مَنْ وَالَاهُ وَ عَادِ مَنْ عَادَاهُ

Whomsoever I am his master, this ʿAlī is also his master. O' Allah! Befriend one who befriends him (ʿAlī), and oppose one who opposes him (ʿAlī).

The angel of revelation, Jibrāʾīl ؑ once again descended by the order of Allah and this time, revealed the following verse of the Quran to the Prophet ﷺ:

﴿أَلْيَوْمَ أَكْمَلْتُ لَكُمْ دِينَكُمْ وَ أَتْمَمْتُ عَلَيْكُمْ نِعْمَتِي وَ رَضِيتُ لَكُمُ الإِسْلَامَ دِيناً﴾

On this day have I completed your religion for you and perfected My bounties upon you and am pleased with Islām as being your religion.[2]

Therefore, this day was marked in history as a momentous and grand day.

The day of *Ghadīr* was a day of epic proportions in history. It was a day which would become known as the day of mastership;

[2] Quran, Sūrah al-Māʾidah (5), verse 3.

the day of leadership; the day of brotherhood; the day of valour; the day of courage, bravery and protection (of the faith); the day of pleasure for the believers; and the day of candidness.

In summary, it was the day of Islām, Quran, and the Ahlul Bayt ﷺ – with the Commander of the Faithful (*Amīr al-Muʾminīn*) and the Leader of the Pious (*Imām al-Muttaqīn*) being the prime focus and centre of attraction - ʿAlī the son of Abī Ṭālib.

It is a day which the followers of the true teachings of the faith of Islam mark with great esteem, and a day when they congratulate one another.

It can be understood from the *aḥādīth* that the Imams of the Ahlul Bayt ﷺ took this day as one of celebration and used to hold special programs to celebrate this event.

It has been narrated from Fayyāḍ b. Muḥammad al-Ṭūsī that: I was in the presence of the eighth Imam [Imam ʿAlī b. Mūsā al-Riḍā] on the day of *Ghadīr* (18th of Dhūl Ḥijjah). I saw a particular group of people serving the Imam and the Imam was (intentionally) keeping them in his house until the time of sunset so that he may give them food to eat (and thus enable them to break their fast). The Imam ordered that food, new clothes, shoes, rings, and other gifts be sent for their families. In the house, I noticed that the state of all of those present was something completely different than normal, and it was from those people that I learned the greatness and magnitude of this day.[3]

In another *ḥadīth* it has been mentioned that one day during the days of the "open caliphate" of Imam ʿAlī ﷺ, the day of *jumuʿah* and *ʿEīd al-Ghadīr* fell together. On this day, the Imam ﷺ delivered a long speech and said:

---

[3] *Biḥār al-Anwār*, v. 97, p. 112, trad. 8.

This gathering shall soon come to an end and all of you will go back to your homes and families – may Allah shower His mercy upon you all.

On this day, you should be [extra] kind to your families and do good deeds to your brothers. You should thank Allah for the blessings which He has granted you. You must also be sure to unite with one another so that through this, Allah may assist you.

Do good to others so Allah makes your friendships firm and immovable. From the blessings which Allah has given you, give gifts to one another. On this day, Allah will give rewards (to you) in multiple folds compared to other days of celebration. This form of reward cannot be attained except through this day (*Ghadīr*). Doing good to others and giving away much wealth to others will increase the life span. Being a host to people will result in the mercy and love of Allah descending upon you.

On this day, as much as you are able to, give your brothers and family a portion of the wealth which Allah has given to you.

Always be smiling and in a happy mood when you meet one another; and be sure to thank Allah for the blessings which He has showered upon you.

Go towards those people whose hope may lie in you and be kind to them. In regards to your food and drink (on this day), ensure that between you and those who are under your care and supervision, there is equality. This equality and equity must be displayed to the extent of your ability (and you should know that) the reward of giving one *dirham* of charity on this day is equivalent to giving 100,000 *dirhams* of charity (on any other day) and the Divine bounty of this is in Allah's Hands alone.

Allah has also made it highly recommended to fast on this day and has promised a great reward for one who observes it. If a person was to look after the needs and necessities of his brothers, even before his own wishes and desires (were expressed to Allah), and if one was to look after their requests in the best possible way, then one will be granted such a reward that it would be equivalent to fasting the entire day and spending the entire night in worship until the morning hours.

A person who feeds another fasting person on this day will be equal to that person who went person by person and fed all of the fasting people (with one's own hands).

You must convey all which you have just heard to those who are not here. The strong and able people must go out in search of the weak people; the powerful must go in search of the oppressed; as these are all things which the Prophet ﷺ commanded me to do.

Imam ʿAlī then read the sermon for *jumuʿah* and performed the *ṣalāt al-jumuʿah* (since there is no special *ṣalāt* for this *ʿeīd*). He then went with his children and Shīʿa to the house of Imam Ḥusain, where food was ready, and he distributed gifts to the Shīʿa – both the needy and even those free from need – who had accompanied him, and then instructed them to go home to their families.[4]

It stands to reason that such a day so important in the history of Islam is something which must be remembered and celebrated for it is a day which saw the perfection of Islam – as if up until that point in time, although Muslims were praying, fasting,

[4] *Biḥār al-Anwār*, vol. 97, Page 117

giving charity, defending their territory and performing all of the other recommended and obligatory actions brought by the Prophet ﷺ, however their submission to Allah was still incomplete; and it was only with the Divinely ordained leadership of Imam ʿAlī b. Abī Ṭālib ؑ that Islam was perfected. Over the twenty-three years of the Prophetic mission and everything which Allah had given to the fledgling Muslim community and all of the bounties and blessings which He had conferred upon them that still He had more to give – He had yet to "complete" His blessings on this new faith of Islam and its followers.

Indeed, it was with the event of Ghadīr al-Khumm that the religion of Islam was perfected, and the never-ending blessings of Allah were completed.

This makes it clear that the crystalization of the Islamic identity of the Muslims then and up until the end of time is through the recognition, acceptance and unwavering support of Imam ʿAlī b. Abī Ṭālib ؑ and his progeny; and that as Muslims, just like Allah took to His book to cement this ideal, the Muslims are also indebted and obligated to proclaim this unique gift and blessing through the actions of the faith.

As for the character and personality of Imam ʿAlī ؑ, he is a man who needs no introduction. It is not only the Muslims of all persuasions who love and adore him, but even non-Muslims have a respect and admiration for this man – people such as the late George Jordac, a Lebanese Christian, who wrote the famous book in Arabic, *Al-Imām ʿAlī Ṣawt al-ʿAdālah al-Insāniyya – Imam ʿAlī: The Voice of Human Justice* - which has been translated into English; or the late Christian author, Sulayman al-Kattani and his work *Al-Imam ʿAlī: Nibrās, Mitrās,* translated and published in English as *Imam Ali: Source of Light, Wisdom and Might;* as well as non-Shia scholars such as the well-known Dr. ʿAdnān Ibrāhīm and his multiple lectures and videos found on YouTube.

But even before them, the Prophet of Islam ﷺ conferred upon him accolades and a unique status; not to mention Allah ﷻ who has Himself dedicated hundreds of verses in the Quran to speak in glowing tributes about a man who is considered as being the 'self' of the Prophet.

Those interested in seeing ʿAlī b. Abī Ṭālib ؑ in the Quran can refer to books such as *Shawāhid al-Tanzīl li Qawāʿīd al-Tafḍīl fī al-Ayāt al-Nāzilah fī Ahl al-Bayt ṣalawātu Allahi wa salāmahu ʿalayhim,* written by a famous Sunni scholar, ʿUbaydullah b. ʿAbd Allah b. Aḥmad al-Ḥaskani al-Nayshabūrī.

This work investigates (albeit at a very rudimentary level), "how" the name of Imam ʿAlī ؑ made it into the *adhān* – is it an innovation (*bidʿah*) or a religious ordiance that we are expected to implement?

The work starts out by addressing this question as responded to by the scholars at **www.IslamQuest.net**. In it, the reader will better understand some aspects on the history of the *adhān* and *iqāmah* and how there have been 'alterations' in these two acts of worship – which as we know are *tawqifī* – actions which have been legislated by Allah – and the stark difference between the various Muslim schools in their practical implementation of them.

From there, we review the opinions of over twenty scholars of the Shīʿa tradition – both those who have passed away and contemporary living scholars – as to what their legally binding ruling (*fatwā*) is on this topic.

We also present a complete set of rulings as issued by His Eminence, Āyatullāh al-Uẓmā al-Ḥājj al-Sayyid ʿAlī al-Ḥusaynī al-Sīstānī from his recently published and fully expanded manual of Islamic laws, *Tawḍīḥ al-Masāʾil Jāmīʿ* in which he details the rulings for the *adhān* and the *iqāmah.*

We close by also presenting some of the recommended supplications which can be recited during and after the call to prayer.

Needless to say that there are lengthy treatises written on this topic analysing the *aḥādīth* literature and the opinions of our scholars from the earliest days of Islamic history, however our goal in this short work was merely to bring forth some basics in this area, and hopefully spark the curiosity of the readers for themselves to seek out deeper academic discourses on this topic.

We are grateful to all of those who offered their support to us during the course of this work, especially our editor, and my wife, Sr. Arifa Hudda, for her review of this work. May Allah reward her for her continuous efforts.

In closing, if after reading this work, you feel that you have benefited from its contents, please keep us in your prayers and ask Allah to continue to shower us with His blessings and bounties.

وَأَمَّا بِنِعْمَةِ رَبِّكَ فَحَدِّثْ

Then as for the blessings and favours
of your Lord, keep on proclaiming them.
Quran, Sūrah al-Ḍuḥā (93), verse 11

Saturday March 31st, 2018 • Rajab 13th, 1439
Birth Anniversary of Imam ʿAlī b. Abī Ṭālib

Saleem Bhimji
Kitchener, Ontario, Canada

Question

How did Prophet Muḥammad ﷺ himself enunciate the *adhān*? Did he testify to his own Prophethood and to the mastership (*wilāyah*) of Imam ʿAlī ؑ within the *adhān*? In addition, why do the Shīʿa mention the phrase: 'I bear witness that ʿAlī is the *walī* of Allah' in the *adhān* and *iqāmah*, and also in the *talqīn* portion during a funeral? Finally we see that Imam ʿAlī ؑ has said: 'Everyone should testify to the Imam of his time.' If he said this, then why do we not testify to the Imam of our time during the *adhān* and *iqāmah*?

Concise Answer to this Question

1. According to narrations, it is certain that the Prophet of Islam ﷺ testified to his own Prophethood in the *adhān* and *iqāmah*, because the Prophet ﷺ just like other people, must act according to the religious rules and ordinances - unless there is a specific time or reason in which the Prophet ﷺ was told that he did not have to follow a particular ruling, and we do not have such an instance for the *adhān*. On the contrary, we have many

narrations that when the Prophet ﷺ recited the *adhān* himself, he testified to the oneness of Allah ﷻ and his own Prophethood.

2. There is no evidence that explicitly indicates that Prophet Muḥammad ﷺ testified to the mastership of Imam ʿAlī (a) in the *adhān*. In addition, in regards to the traditions that have been quoted from the Imams of the Ahlul Bayt (a) in which they have expressed the components of the *adhān* in detail, they have not mentioned the third testimony (testimony to the mastership of Imam ʿAlī (a)), although there are many traditions (concerning other than the *adhān*) in which the specific rewards have been conveyed for mentioning the name of Imam ʿAlī (a) after saying the name of the Prophet ﷺ. Therefore, most senior Shīʿa scholars say that since the *adhān* is an act of worship, and since it is possible that the third testimony is not a part of it, it is only permitted to testify to the mastership of ʿAlī (a) with the intention of seeking nearness (to Allah ﷻ) and **not** with the intention of it being a legislated part of the *adhān*.

3. As for the testimony to the Imam of our time (aj), it must be said that from the following *ḥadīth* [which has been referred to in the question although not expressly mentioned] we can conclude that by the infallible Imam saying [in a portion of the *ḥadīth*]:

...مَنْ كَانَ مُقِيماً عَلَى الْإِقْرَارِ بِالْأَئِمَّةِ (ع) كُلِّهِمْ وَ بِإِمَامِ زَمَانِهِ وَ وَلَايَتِهِ...

> ...An individual who is resolved upon testifying to the Imams, peace be upon them, all of them, and upon the Imam of his time and his authority...

that this *ḥadīth* does not give us any indication to the requirement of bearing witness to the leadership of the Imam of the time in the *adhān* - it merely implies that a believer must stay firm on the mastership of the infallible Imams (a) [which can be understood when one reviews the entire *ḥadīth* – which we have not mentioned here].

Detailed Answer to this Question

To better understand this issue, we must first explain a few points:

1. The *adhān* and *iqāmah* are considered as being acts of worship and as such, all acts of worship are *tawqifī* – which means that they are legislated by Allah ﷻ and other than Allah ﷻ and His Messenger ﷺ, no one has the right to legislate and initiate any laws in Islam.

2. One cannot pass judgement or issue a legally-binding ruling (*fatwā*) through reading a *ḥadīth* in one or even several books and then act according to that ruling, because amongst the *aḥādīth*, there are some which are general, and others which are absolute; some which are specific and others which are conditional; some which may conflict with others; while others were issued during a period of dissimulation (*taqiyyah*). Therefore in such cases, the narrations must be given to the experts who have long been familiar with the sciences required to review and authenticate such statements as they are the ones who practice *ijtihād* – derivation of the laws of Islam from the recognized sources – and it is this status which they have achieved that permits them to come to a conclusion on such religious issues.

Since several queries have been raised in this one question, the answers will be presented in a number of sections.

A. Method of the Prophet ﷺ for the Adhān and Iqāmah

According to the narrations, it is certain that the Prophet ﷺ testified to his own Prophethood in the *adhān*, because the Prophet ﷺ must act upon all of the religious ordinances, just like everyone else is expected to do so, unless there is a specific time or specified reason that the Prophet ﷺ does not have to follow a certain religious injunction; and when it comes to the *adhān*, there was no special decree given to him. Rather, we have many narrations that Prophet Muḥammad ﷺ clearly and unequivocally acknowledged the Oneness of Allah and his own status of Prophethood when he recited the *adhān*. Here are some examples of the narratives which speak about this.

Imam Muḥammad al-Bāqir ؑ said:

> On the night of the ascension (*meʿrāj*), when the Prophet arrived at *al-Bayt al-Maʿmūr*,[5] the time of the prayers had set in. The angel Jibrāʾīl ؑ said the *adhān* and *iqāmah* and the Prophet stood in front to lead the prayers, while the angels and previous Prophets stood behind the Prophet (Muḥammad ﷺ) to perform the prayers.

Someone asked Imam al-Bāqir ؑ:

> How did Jibrāʾīl pronounce the *adhān*?

The Imam ؑ replied:

[5] A location in either the 4th or 7th heaven which is directly opposite in direction to the Kaʿbah on earth in which the angels busy themselves with worship and circumambulation. (Tr.)

> [He said] Allah is the Greatest ... I bear witness that there is no god except Allah ... I bear witness that Muḥammad is the Messenger of Allah ... (until the end of the *adhān*).[6]

Thus, it is clear that when the *adhān* has been legislated with these sentences [we have omitted them from the narration, however what is mentioned in the *ḥadīth* is the complete *adhān* which is recited today], the utterances from the Prophet ﷺ when he recites the *adhān* cannot be in a different manner.

Therefore, the way of proclaiming the *adhān* by the Prophet ﷺ is no different from the *adhān* proclaimed by angel Jibrāʾīl ﷺ and the followers within the nation (*ummah*) of the Prophet ﷺ.[7]

In another tradition, Imam al-Ḥusayn ﷺ said: I heard my father ʿAlī b. Abī Ṭālib ﷺ say:

> The Lord sent an angel who took the Prophet on the night ascension (*meʿrāj*). On that journey, there was an angel who had never been seen before in the heavens and after this event, it was never to be seen again, and [it was this angel] who pronounced the *adhān* and the *iqāmah*. When they were both pronounced and completed, the angel Jibrāʾīl said to the Prophet ﷺ: This is the way that you must say the *adhān* for the prayers.[8]

---

[6] Ṭūsī, Muḥammad b. al-Ḥasan, *Tahdhīb al-Aḥkām*, Researched and Edited by Ḥasan Mousavī Khorasān, v. 2, p. 60, Dar al-Kutub al-Islāmiyya, Tehran, Fourth Edition, 1407 AH.

[7] Subḥānī, Jaʿfar, *Al-Iʿtisām bi al-Kitāb wa al-Sunnah*, p. 27, Imam Ṣādiq ﷺ Institute, Qum, First Edition, ND.

[8] Tamimī, Qādī Nūʿmān Muḥammad al-, *Daʿāim al-Islām*, Dār al-Maʿārif, Cairo, v. 1, p. 142.

In addition, we know that the religious injunctions [which come from Allah ﷻ] were sent for all Muslims to follow and the Prophet ﷺ takes priority over everyone in all of the affairs – including the practical implementation of the religious rulings. In this area, there is no difference between him and other people, except in some special rights or duties that exist which are documented [in the Islamic sources] to clarify where he has specific responsibilities.

Therefore, we reiterate the fact that the proclamation of the *adhān* and *iqāmah* of the Prophet ﷺ is the same *adhān* and *iqāmah* which all other people within Islam are also expected to recite.

B. Testimony to the Authority of Imam ʿAlī ؑ in the Adhān, Iqāmah and Talqīn

However, as for the question which was posed that: Did the Prophet ﷺ himself bear witness in his recital of the *adhān* to the mastership (*wilāyah*) of Imam ʿAlī ؑ? Before we can answer this question, it is necessary to first reflect on the meaning of the word "*walī*" and then we will be able to answer this question.

The word "*walī*" can mean a number of things, and the most important definitions are as follows:

1. This word means 'guardianship' and 'one who takes on a responsibility'; just as can be seen in the various verses of the Noble Quran in which the word "*walī*" has been used in the same sense. For example:

﴿اللَّهُ الَّذِي خَلَقَ السَّمَاوَاتِ وَالْأَرْضَ وَمَا بَيْنَهُمَا فِي سِتَّةِ أَيَّامٍ
ثُمَّ اسْتَوَىٰ عَلَى الْعَرْشِ ۖ مَا لَكُم مِّن دُونِهِ مِن وَلِيٍّ وَلَا شَفِيعٍ ۚ
أَفَلَا تَتَذَكَّرُونَ﴾

> God is He who has created the heavens and the earth and what is between them in six days, then established Himself on the Supreme Throne. You have apart from Him, **no guardian (to whom you might refer the ultimate meaning and outcome of your affairs)**, nor any intermediary (who without His leave, can cause anything of use to reach you). Will you not then reflect and be mindful?[9]

2. This word has also been used in the meaning of a 'friend'[10] which is also mentioned in the Quran:

﴿وَلَا تَسْتَوِي الْحَسَنَةُ وَلَا السَّيِّئَةُ ۚ ادْفَعْ بِالَّتِي هِيَ أَحْسَنُ فَإِذَا الَّذِي بَيْنَكَ وَبَيْنَهُ عَدَاوَةٌ كَأَنَّهُ وَلِيٌّ حَمِيمٌ﴾

> Goodness and evil can never be equal. Repel evil with what is better (or best). Then see: the one between whom and you there was enmity has become a **close friend.**[11]

3. It is also used as a helper and assistant[12] as mentioned in the Quran:

﴿وَالْمُؤْمِنُونَ وَالْمُؤْمِنَاتُ بَعْضُهُمْ أَوْلِيَاءُ بَعْضٍ ۚ يَأْمُرُونَ بِالْمَعْرُوفِ وَيَنْهَوْنَ عَنِ الْمُنْكَرِ وَيُقِيمُونَ الصَّلَاةَ وَيُؤْتُونَ

---

[9] Quran, Sūrah al-Sajdah (32), verse 4.

[10] Refer to question 154 found on **www.islamquest.net** concerning the "Meaning of *Wilāyah*" and question 8435 concerning "*Wilāyah* in the Quran and in the opinion of the Ahl al-Sunnah."

[11] Quran, Sūrah al-Fussilat (41), verse 34.

[12] Ibn Manḍhūr, Muḥammad b. Mukarram, *Lisān al-ʿArab*, v. 15, p. 407, Printed by Dār al-Ṣādir, Beirut, Third Edition, 1414 AH.

الزَّكَاةَ وَيُطِيعُونَ اللَّهَ وَرَسُولَهُ أُولَٰئِكَ سَيَرْحَمُهُمُ اللَّهُ إِنَّ اللَّهَ عَزِيزٌ حَكِيمٌ

The believers, both men and women, they are **guardians, confidants, and helpers** of one another. They enjoin and promote what is right and good and forbid and try to prevent the evil, and they establish the prescribed prayer in conformity with its conditions, and pay the prescribed purifying alms. They obey God and His Messenger. They are the ones whom God will treat with mercy. Surely God is All-Glorious with irresistible might, All-Wise.[13]

There is no doubt that the meanings mentioned in the above verses for the term *"walī Allah"* for believers means the second and third definitions (friend and helper); rather, even in the *aḥādīth* of the Ahl al-Sunnah and the Shīʿa, this is also the meaning which has been referred to.[14]

However when specifically talking about the first definition mentioned above, it must be said that there are traditions that state that Imam ʿAlī is the guardian and protector, and the one who takes precedence over the lives of all of the Muslims - just as has been described in regards to the great Prophet of Islam and his status:

---

[13] Quran, Sūrah al-Tawbah (9), verse 71.
[14] Ibn Abī Ḥātim, ʿAbd al-Raḥmān b. Muḥammad, *Tafsīr al-Qurān al-Adhīm*, Researched by Asʿad Muḥammad al-Ṭayyib, v. 2, p. 675, Printed by Maktaba Nizār Muṣṭafā al-Bāz, Third Edition, 1419 AH.

﴿النَّبِيُّ أَوْلَىٰ بِالْمُؤْمِنِينَ مِنْ أَنْفُسِهِمْ ۖ وَأَزْوَاجُهُ أُمَّهَاتُهُمْ ۗ وَأُولُو
الْأَرْحَامِ بَعْضُهُمْ أَوْلَىٰ بِبَعْضٍ فِي كِتَابِ اللَّهِ مِنَ الْمُؤْمِنِينَ
وَالْمُهَاجِرِينَ إِلَّا أَنْ تَفْعَلُوا إِلَىٰ أَوْلِيَائِكُمْ مَعْرُوفًا ۚ كَانَ ذَٰلِكَ
فِي الْكِتَابِ مَسْطُورًا﴾

> The Prophet has a higher claim [*awlā*] on the believers than they have on their own selves, and (seeing that he is as a father to them), his wives are (as) their mothers. Those who are bound by blood have a greater right (in inheritance and charity) upon one another according to God's Book than other believers and the emigrants – except that you must (nevertheless) act with kindness toward your friends (and bequeath some of your goods to them). That is what is written in the Book (of God's Decree).[15]

Of course Imam ʿAlī is the *walī* of Allah - that is - he has been appointed by the Lord as the chief and guardian of the entire Muslim nation, just like when it is said that Muḥammad is the Messenger of Allah [*Muḥammadan Rasūlullah*] – by this we mean that Prophet Muḥammad has been appointed to the position of Messengership by Allah.

Going back to the discussion, there is no clear evidence that explicitly indicates that Prophet Muḥammad testified to the mastership of Imam ʿAlī in his *adhān*. Although it is written in *al-Salāfah al-Khilāfah* that Salmān al-Muḥammadī (al-Fārsī) added the third testimony in his recitation of the *adhān* and this caused a man to go to the Prophet and complain to him about

[15] Quran, Sūrah al-Aḥzāb (33), verse 6.

what he heard, however the Noble Prophet ﷺ replied to this man saying: "You have heard a good word."

It is also stated in this same book (*al-Salāfah al-Khilāfah*) that after the event of *Ghadīr*, Abū Dharr al-Ghiffārī also testified to the authority of the Commander of the Faithful ʿAlī ؑ in his recitation of the *adhān* after bearing witness to the Oneness of Allah and the Prophethood of Prophet Muḥammad ﷺ, and as a group of hypocrites did not like what they heard, they went to the Prophet ﷺ to protest about this. The Prophet ﷺ replied to them saying:

أَمَّا وَعَيْتُمْ خُطْبَتِي يَوْمَ الْغَدِيرِ لِعَلِيٍّ بِالْوَلَايَةِ.

In essence, what the Prophet ﷺ said to them was: "What was that lengthy sermon all about that I delivered to you all on the scorching desert heat on the Day of *Ghadīr*? Was the meaning of that sermon anything other than the fact that Imam ʿAlī, the Commander of the Faithful, is the representative of Allah [during my life and after my death]?"

The Prophet ﷺ then said to these hypocrites:

> Have you not heard me say that the sky has not covered over, nor has the earth given its place to anyone who is more truthful than Abū Dharr!?[16]

However with that said, firstly the book referenced (*al-Salāfah al-Khilāfah*) is not available to further investigate the chain of narrators of this *ḥadīth*; and secondly such a narrative has not been found in any of the texts which date back before the 7th century so as to allow us to comment on its chain of narrators.

---

[16] Murāghi, Shaykh ʿAbd Allah al-, *Al-Salāfah fī amr al-Khilāfah*, pp. 32-33; Manuscript; Al-Murāghī is a scholar from the Ahl as-Sunnah who lived in the 7th century; his book is one of the manuscripts which is still available in the Dhāhiriyya Library in Damascus.

In addition to the narrations that have been quoted from the infallible Imams in regards to the specific lines which make up the *adhān*, there is no mention of the testimony to the mastership of Imam ʿAlī. Therefore, when we look at the traditions, we do see statements which explain the actual individual components which made up the *adhān* during the time of the Prophet ﷺ. As such, according to the narrations from the Ahlul Bayt, the *adhān* has eighteen sentences and they are as follows:[17]

أَللهُ أَكْبَرُ

أَللهُ أَكْبَرُ

أَللهُ أَكْبَرُ

أَللهُ أَكْبَرُ

أَشْهَدُ أَنْ لَا إِلٰهَ إِلَّا اللهُ

أَشْهَدُ أَنْ لَا إِلٰهَ إِلَّا اللهُ

أَشْهَدُ أَنَّ مُحَمَّداً رَسُولُ اللهِ

أَشْهَدُ أَنَّ مُحَمَّداً رَسُولُ اللهِ

حَيَّ عَلَىٰ الصَّلَاةِ

حَيَّ عَلَىٰ الصَّلَاةِ

حَيَّ عَلَىٰ الْفَلَاحِ

[17] Qummī, Abū Jaʿfar Muḥammd b. ʿAlī b. Bābāwayya al-, *Man lā Yaḥdhuruhu al-Faqīh*, v. 1, pp. 289-290, Jamīʿ al-Mudarrisīn, Qum, 1413 AH; *Tahdhīb al-Aḥkām*, v. 2, p. 61.

حَيَّ عَلَىٰ الْفَلَاحِ

حَيَّ عَلَىٰ خَيْرِ الْعَمَلِ

حَيَّ عَلَىٰ خَيْرِ الْعَمَلِ

أَللّٰهُ أَكْبَرُ

أَللّٰهُ أَكْبَرُ

لَا إِلٰهَ إِلَّا اللّٰهُ

لَا إِلٰهَ إِلَّا اللّٰهُ

However, there are many traditions regarding the reward of bearing testimony to the mastership of Imam ʿAlī ☪ by saying: "I bear witness that ʿAlī is the *walī* of Allah" - after the testimony to the Oneness of Allah ﷻ and the Prophethood of Prophet Muḥammad ﷺ, and we will quote a few examples which are worthy of mentioning below:

Imam al-Ṣādiq ☪ says:

> After the creation of the heavens and the earth, Allah, the Exalted, commanded a caller that he might call out these three testimonies.[18]

Please note that this "caller" was a reference to the response of those who existed in the previous world (*ʿālam al-dharr*), just as Imam al-Ṣādiq ☪ has said under the commentary of the verse:

---

[18] Kulaynī, Muḥammad b. Yaʿqūb, *Al-Kāfī*, Researched and Edited by: ʿAlī Akbar Ghaffārī, and Muḥammad Ākhundī, v. 1, p. 441, Dar al-Kutub al-Islāmiyyah, Tehran, Fourth Edition, 1407 AH; Shaykh al-Ṣadūq, *al-Amālī*, p. 604, Aʿlāmī Printing House, Beirut, Fifth Edition, 1400 AH.

﴿وَإِذْ أَخَذَ رَبُّكَ مِنْ بَنِي آدَمَ مِنْ ظُهُورِهِمْ ذُرِّيَّتَهُمْ وَأَشْهَدَهُمْ عَلَىٰ أَنْفُسِهِمْ أَلَسْتُ بِرَبِّكُمْ ۖ قَالُوا بَلَىٰ ۛ شَهِدْنَا ۛ أَنْ تَقُولُوا يَوْمَ الْقِيَامَةِ إِنَّا كُنَّا عَنْ هَٰذَا غَافِلِينَ﴾

> And (remember O Messenger) when your Lord brought forth from the children of Adam, from their loins, their offspring, and made them bear witness against themselves (asking them:) 'Am I not your Lord?' They said: 'Yes, we do bear witness. (That covenant was taken) lest you should say on the Day of Resurrection, We were indeed unaware of this (fact that you are our Lord).'[19]

In this regards, Imam al-Ṣādiq ﷺ has said:

> Allah, the Exalted, took from the loins of humanity all of the zygotes that would ever come into existence on earth and introduced Himself (through the manifestation of His essence). If this event was not one in which He introduced Himself and His Divine Essence to all of the people who would come in the future, then no one would have ever known their Lord. Then Allah asked [them all]: 'Am I not your Lord?' All of them said: 'We confirm [that You are our Lord].' Allah then said: 'Then know that this Muhammad is My Messenger, and ʿAlī, the Commander of the Faithful, is the successor and protector (of the Prophet).'[20]

---

[19] Quran, Sūrah al-Aʿrāf (7), verse 172.

[20] Ṣaffār, Muḥammad b. Ḥasan, *Baṣāʾir al-Darajāt fī fadhāʾil Āl Muḥammad ṣalla Allahu ʿalayhim*, Researched and Edited by Moḥsen

Additionally, it has been mentioned by Imam al-Ṣādiq ﷺ as well that:

> When Allah created the *ʿarsh*, the *kursī* and ... He wrote on them:
>
> لَا إِلٰهَ إِلَّا اللّٰهُ، مُحَمَّدٌ رَسُولُ اللّٰهِ، عَلِيٌّ أَمِيرُ الْمُؤْمِنِينَ
>
> There is no god except for Allah; Muḥammad is the Messenger of Allah; ʿAlī is the Commander of the Faithful.
>
> Therefore, anytime one of you says: 'There is no god except for Allah and Muḥammad is the Messenger of Allah', (after this) you must also say: '"ʿAlī is the Commander of the Faithful.'[21]

From such Prophetic narratives we also can conclude that: bearing witness to the mastership of Imam ʿAlī ﷺ after bearing witness to the unity of Allah ﷻ and the Prophetic role of Muḥammad al-Muṣṭafa ﷺ is not only permissible but it is something loved by Allah ﷻ. Ibn Abbas has quoted the Prophet ﷺ in which he said:

> I swear by Allah who sent me as a Prophet! The *ʿarsh*, *kursi*, the celestial planes, the heavens, and the earth do not stay in their place except that upon them it is written: 'There is no god except for Allah, Muḥammad

b. ʿAbbas ʿAlī Kuche Vāghī, v.1, p. 71, Ayatullah al-Marʿashī al-Najafī Library, Qum, Second Edition, 1404 AH; Furāt b. Ibrāhīm, *Tafsīr Furāt al-Kūfī*, Researched and Edited by Muḥammad Kādhim, pp. 148-149, Al-Ṭabʿ wa al-Nashr fī Wizārah al-Irshād al-Islāmī, Tehran, First Edition, 1410 AH.

[21] Ṭabrsī, Aḥmad b. ʿAlī, *Al-Iḥtijāj ʿalā ahl al-Lijāj*, Researched and Edited by Muḥammad Bāqir Khorasān, v. 1, p. 158, Murtaḍā Publishers, Mashad, First Edition, 1403 AH.

> is the Messenger of Allah, and ʿAlī is the Commander of the Faithful.'[22]

However, since the *adhān* is an act worship, and it is likely that bearing witness to the mastership of the Commander of the Faithful ﷺ is not a part of this act of worship, and most Shīʿa jurists do not consider it as a part of the *adhān,*[23] but they do state that if it is read for the sake of seeking nearness to Allah ﷻ or to seek His blessings, and **not** with the intention of being a legislated part of the *adhān*, then it is permissible.[24]

Ultimately, the doubt which may be brought up at this point is that it may be stated that saying this line in the *adhān* or *iqāmah* may be considered as an innovation in the religion (*bidʿa*).

However, the meaning of innovation is:

> Inserting a belief or practice in the realm of religion without any reference of it being mentioned in the religious sources, such as the Quran and the traditions of the infallibles ﷺ.

---

[22] *Biḥār al-Anwār*, v. 27, p. 8; Muḥammad b. Ḥasan Ḥurr al-ʿĀmulī, *Al-Jawāhir al-Siniyyah fī al-Aḥādīth al-Qudsiyyah* (*Kulliyāt Ḥadīth Qudsī*), p. 587, Intishārāt Dehqān, Tehran, Third Edition, 1422 AH.

[23] Although a group of jurists do regard it as being a part of the *adhān* and have stated that it is recommended (*mustaḥab*) to be said – refer to *Biḥār al-Anwār*, v. 81, p. 111; Sayyid Muḥammad Ḥusaynī Shīrāzī, *Min Fiqh al-Zahrā' alayhā al-salām*, v. 3, pg. 144, Rashid Publishers, Qum, First Printing, 1428 AH; Muḥammad Sanad al-Baḥrānī, *Al-Shahādah al-Thālitha*, Reviewed by ʿAlī Shukrī Baghdādī, pp. 43-46, ND.

[24] Khomeinī, Sayyid Rūḥullah al-Musawī, *Tawḍīḥ al-Masā'il* with notes, v. 1, p. 519, Daftar Intashārāt Islāmī, Qum, Eighth Edition, 1424 AH.

Since this is the clear and accepted definition of what a religious innovation is,[25] we categorically state that if someone considers this line [about the mastership of ʿAlī ﷺ] which is read in the *adhān* or *iqāmah* as a part of the *adhān*, then this is an innovation in the religion and is something forbidden (*ḥarām*).

But given that most of the Shīʿa jurists **do not** consider this line as a **part** of the *adhān*, and they clearly state that if it is said in the *adhān* or *iqāmah*, then it must not be said in a way which would mimic the lines of the *adhān* or *iqāmah,* then it does not fall into the realm of impermissibility.

Therefore, it is not an innovation and it is not a problem to then say this line in the *adhān* and the *iqāmah.*

In any case, the rationale behind why a majority of the Shīʿite jurists say that the recitation of the third testimony in the *adhān* or *iqāmah* is permissible so long as it is recited without considering it to be a part of the *adhān* or *iqāmah* is that the above mentioned traditions clearly state that:

> Whenever you testify to the belief of monotheism and the messengership of the Prophet ﷺ, then you must also testify to the mastership of ʿAlī b. Abī Ṭālib ؑ.

Since such traditions are unconditional – meaning that they are not restricted, therefore they include the state of *adhān* and *iqāmah* and even outside of the *adhān* and *iqāmah*, and this is what is meant by the statement that they are not a part of the overall lines which are read in the *adhān.*

---

[25] Rāghib Iṣfahānī, Ḥusayn b. Muḥammad, *al-Mufradāt fī Gharīb al-Quran*, Researched by ʿAdnān Ṣafwān Dāwūdī, p. 111, Dār al-ʿIlm, Al-Dār al-Shāmiyyah, Damascus, Beirut, First Edition, 1412 AH; Maḥmūd ʿAbd al-Raḥmān, *Muʿjam al-Muṣṭalaḥāt wa al-Fādh al-Fiqhiyya*, v. 1, pp. 361-362, ND.

As a result, saying the sentence "ʿAlī is the *walī* of Allah" in the *adhān*, *iqāmah*, and *talqīn*, by keeping in the forefront of the mind, the rank and position of Imam ʿAlī 🕊[26] - if this is done with the intention of seeking spiritual proximity to Allah 🕊 and as a form of pursuing the benedictions and blessings, and if it is done with the understanding that it is not a legislated portion of these recitations, then it is not a problem.

It is noteworthy that in some Sunni sources[27] it has been mentioned that one time, the *muaddhin* (a person who recites the *adhān*) went to ʿUmar b. al-Khaṭṭāb to wake him up for the *fajr* prayers and found him deep in sleep and so he said to him:

أَلصَّلاَةُ خَيْرٌ مِنَ النَّوْمِ

Prayer (*ṣalāt*) is better than sleep!

When ʿUmar eventually woke up and heard this line, he then ordered that this sentence be added to the *adhān* for the morning (*fajr*) prayers.[28]

This practice continues until today and this is why the Ahl as-Sunnah have added this line into their *adhān* and say it immediately after:

حَىَّ عَلَىٰ الْفَلَاحِ

Hasten towards success.

---

[26] Questions from www.islamquest.net – "Proving the Imāmate of Imam ʿAlī 🕊" - question 999; see also: "Proving the Imāmate of Imam ʿAlī 🕊 from the Quran" - question 324.

[27] See Appendix I for a screen captures which speak about this. (Tr.)

[28] al-Aṣbaḥī, Mālik b. Anas b. Mālik b. Abī ʿĀmir b. ʿAmr b. al-Ḥārith b. Ghaymān b. Khuthayn b. ʿAmr b. al-Ḥārith, *al-Muwaṭṭa'*, *Bāb al-Nidā' li ṣalāh*; Ibn Abi Shayba, Ḥāfiẓ ʿAbd Allāh b. Muḥammad, *Muṣnaf b. Abī Shayba fī al-aḥādīth wa al-Āthār*, v. 1, p. 236, Dār al-Fikr, Beirut.

Who was it amongst the Ahl as-Sunnah that permitted the repetition of this line in the *adhān* of the morning prayers!? Is it really possible to compare this line and the innovation in the 'Sunni' *adhān* with the mastership (*wilāyah*) of Imam ʿAlī ﵇ in the 'Shīʿa' *adhān* – which once again we repeat that the Shīʿa clearly say is NOT a part of the *adhān*?!

C. Bearing Witness to Imam al-Zāman ﷺ in the *Adhān*

The issue which was also brought up in this question was in regards to bearing witness to the Imam of the time in the *adhān*. Apparently this question has come out of the fact that there is a tradition, a portion of which, says:

...مَنْ كَانَ مُقِيماً عَلَى الْإِقْرَارِ بِالْأَئِمَّةِ ﵈ كُلِّهِمْ وَ بِإِمَامِ زَمَانِهِ وَ وَلَايَتِهِ...

> ...An individual who is resolved upon testifying to the Imams, peace be upon them, all of them, and upon the Imam of his time and his authority...[29]

However this *ḥadīth* does not imply or indicate towards bearing witness or testimony to the Imam of the time ﷺ in the context of the *adhān*; rather, it implies the need to maintain an unwavering belief on the part of the believers in regards to the mastership and authority of the infallible Imams ﵈.

[29] *Biḥār al-Anwār*, v. 80, p. 47, Al-Wafā' Institute; Beirut, 1404 AH.

Appendix I

Innovation in the 'Sunni' Adhān

On www.muwatta.com/the-adhan-for-subh/30, the following has been mentioned:

The Adhan for Subh

Admin July 31, 2015 Comments Off on The Adhan for Subh

> *Yahya related to me from Malik that he had heard that the Muadhdhin came to 'Umar ibn al-Khattab to call him to the Subh {morning} prayer and found him sleeping, so he said:*
>
> *"Prayer is better than sleep," and 'Umar ordered him to put that in the Adhan for Subh.*
>
> وَحَدَّثَنِي عَنْ مَالِكٍ، أَنَّهُ بَلَغَهُ أَنَّ الْمُؤَذِّنَ، جَاءَ إِلَى عُمَرَ بْنِ الْخَطَّابِ يُؤْذِنُهُ لِصَلاَةِ الصُّبْحِ فَوَجَدَهُ نَائِمًا فَقَالَ الصَّلاَةُ خَيْرٌ مِنَ النَّوْمِ . فَأَمَرَهُ عُمَرُ أَنْ يَجْعَلَهَا فِي نِدَاءِ الصُّبْحِ
>
> *{Muwatta of Imam Malik ~ Book 3, Hadith #154}*

~ May Allah be well pleased with them

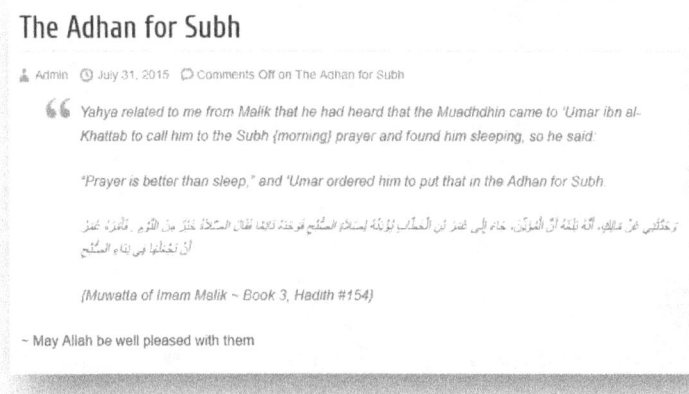

On www.ahadith.co.uk/chapter.php?cid=2331, the following has been mentioned:

Hadith No: 8
Narrated/Authority of

Yahya related to me from Malik that he had heard that the muadhdhin came to Umar ibn al-Khattab to call him to the subh prayer and found him sleeping, so he said, "Prayer is better than sleep," and Umar ordered him to put that in the adhan for subh.

Report Mistake | Permalink

---

30 Last accessed on March 21, 2018.
31 Ibid.

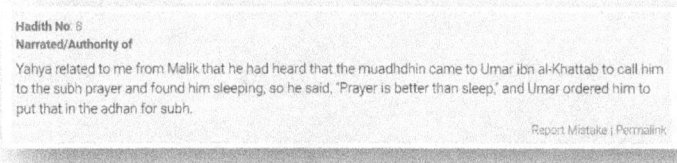

Fatāwā of the Major Shīʿa Scholars

What follows is the rulings of the contemporary and previous senior scholars (*al-Marājiʿ al-Taqlīd*) and their religious edicts as to the mentioning of the mastership of ʿAlī b. Abī Ṭālib in the *adhān*.

All scholars mentioned in the follow section are presented in alphabetical order by way of their last name.

We have maintained the original ruling in Farsi for reference of the readers, as well as their English translations and as far as possible, we ensured that these rulings were from the most recent electronic version of their *Islamic Laws* manual published on their respective websites.

1. Āyatullāh al-ʿUẓmā Shaykh Jawādī Āmulī

مساله ۲۴۳: اشهد أن علي ولي الله جزء اذان و اقامه نیست و مناسب است به عنوان تبرك و تيمن بعد از أشهد أن محمداً رسول الله گفته شود.

Ruling 243: The phrase, 'I bear witness that indeed ʿAlī is the *walī* of Allah' - "أَشْهَدُ أَنَّ عَلِيّاً وَلِيُّ اللهِ" is not a part of the *adhān* or *iqāmah*, and it is proper to say it after saying: 'I bear witness that Muhammad is the Messenger of Allah' - "أَشْهَدُ أَنَّ مُحَمَّداً رَسُولُ اللهِ" as [a form of seeking] Divine blessings and benedictions.

2. Āyatullāh al-ʿUẓmā Sayyid ʿAbdul Karīm Mūsawī Ardebilī

گفتن شهادت ثالثه در اذان و اقامه، به عنوان جزئيت جايز نيست؛ ولى گفتن در اذان و اقامه، به قصد قربت مطلقه، خوب است.

Reply to a Question: Pronouncing the third testimony - 'I bear witness that indeed ʿAlī is the *walī* of Allah' - [أَشْهَدُ أَنَّ عَلِيّاً وَلِيُّ اللهِ] in the *adhān* and *iqāmah* if done with the intention that it is a part of them is not permissible, however saying it in the *adhān* or *iqāmah* with the intention of seeking nearness [to Allah] is ok.

3. Āyatullāh al-ʿUẓmā Sayyid ʿAlavī Gurgānī

«أَشْهَدُ أَنَّ عَلِيّاً وَلِيُّ اللّهِ» جزء اذان واقامه نيست، ولي خوب است بعد از «أَشْهَدُأَنَّ مُحَمَّداً رَسُولُ اللّه»، به قصد قربت گفته شود.

Ruling 928: The phrase - 'I bear witness that indeed ʿAlī is the *walī* of Allah' - "أَشْهَدُ أَنَّ عَلِيّاً وَلِيُّ اللهِ" is not a part of the *adhān* and *iqāmah*, however it is better that it be said after: 'I bear witness that Muhammad is the Messenger of Allah' - "أَشْهَدُ أَنَّ مُحَمَّداً رَسُولُ اللهِ" with the intention of seeking nearness [to Allah].

4. Āyatullāh al-ʿUẓmā Shaykh Nūrī Hamadānī

اشهدً انّ علياً وليّ اللهِ جزء اذان و اقامه نيست ولي خوب است بعد از اشهدً انّ محمداً رسولُ اللهِ، به قصد قربت گفته شود. و چون در امثال زمان ما، شعار تشيع محسوب مي شود در هر جا كه اظهار اين شعار مستحسن و لازم باشد، گفتن آن هم مستحسن و لازم است.

Ruling 920: The phrase - 'I bear witness that indeed ʿAlī is the *walī* of Allah' - "أَشْهَدُ أَنَّ عَلِيّاً وَلِيُّ اللهِ" is not a part of the *adhān* and *iqāmah,* however it is good to say it after: 'I bear witness that Muhammad is the Messenger of Allah' - "أَشْهَدُ أَنَّ مُحَمَّداً رَسُولُ اللهِ" with the intention of seeking nearness [to Allah]. In addition, as in an era like ours, this phrase has become a slogan for the Shīʿa and [as we know] expressing this slogan in any occasion is something which is suitable and actually required, thus saying this line [within the context of the *adhān* and *iqāmah*] is also suitable and required.

5. Āyatullāh al-ʿUẓmā Sayyid ʿAlī Ḥusaynī Khāmeneʾī

گفتن «أشهد أنّ علياً ولي الله» به عنوان شعار تشيع خوب و مهم است و بايد به قصد قربت مطلقه گفته شود، ولى جزو اذان و اقامه نيست.

Ruling 456: Saying - 'I bear witness that indeed ʿAlī is the *walī* of Allah' - "أَشْهَدُ أَنَّ عَلِيّاً وَلِيُّ اللهِ" is a slogan of the Shīʿa is something good [to do] and is important and must be said with the intention of seeking nearness [to Allah], however it is not a part of the *adhān* or *iqāmah.*

6. Āyatullāh al-ʿUẓmā Shaykh Waḥīd Khurasānī

«اَشْهَدُ اَنَّ عَلِيا وَلِى اللّهِ» جزء اذان و اقامه نيست ، ولى چون ولايت آن حضرت مكمّل دين است ، شهادت به آن در هر حال و از جمله بعد از «اَشْهَدُ اَنَّ مُحَمَّداً رَسُولُ اللّهِ» از أفضل قُربات است.

Ruling 928: The phrase - 'I bear witness that indeed ʿAlī is the *walī* of Allah' - "أَشْهَدُ أَنَّ عَلِيّاً وَلِيُّ اللهِ" is not a part of the *adhān* and *iqāmah,* however as his *wilayah* (mastership and authority) forms the completion of the religion [of Islam], thus testifying to that in any state and [specifically] after: 'I bear witness that Muhammad is the Messenger of Allah' - "أَشْهَدُ أَنَّ مُحَمَّداً رَسُولُ اللهِ" is the best of ways to attain proximity [to Allah].

7. Āyatullāh al-ʿUẓmā Shaykh Ḥusayn Mazāherī

«أَشْهَدُ أَنَّ عَلِيّاً وَلِيُّ اللّهِ» جزو اذان و اقامه نيست ولى مستحب است بعد از «أَشْهَدُ أَنَّ مُحَمَداً رَسُولُ اللّهِ»، دو مرتبه گفته شود (مستحب در مستحب)، لكن چون فعلاً شعار شيعه است، بايد گفته شود.

Ruling 729: The phrase - 'I bear witness that indeed ʿAlī is the *walī* of Allah' - "أَشْهَدُ أَنَّ عَلِيّاً وَلِيُّ اللهِ" is not a part of the *adhān* and *iqāmah*, however it is recommended (*mustahab*) that after: 'I bear witness that Muhammad is the Messenger of Allah' - "أَشْهَدُ أَنَّ مُحَمَّداً رَسُولُ اللهِ" that this line is stated twice (a recommended act within a recommended act) – rather presently, this phrase is a slogan of the Shīʿa, and it must be said.

8. Āyatullāh al-ʿUẓmā Sayyid Taqī Modarresī

فقها گفته اند که شهادت سوم (اشهد ان علياً ولي الله) جزء اذان و اقامه نيست ولي شهادت به رسالت حضرت ختمی مرتبت را کامل می کند و امروزه شعار شيعيان شده است. بنابراین اولی آن است که به قصد رجاء مطلوبیت گفته شود.

Ruling 103: The jurists have stated that the third testimony - 'I bear witness that indeed 'Alī is the *walī* of Allah' - "أَشْهَدُ أَنَّ عَلِيّاً وَلِيُّ اللهِ" is not a part of the *adhān* and *iqāmah*, however this phrase completes the testimony to the messsengership of the Final Prophet, and today this phrase has become a slogan of the Shīʿa. Therefore, it is advisable than it is read with the intention of attaining proximity (to Allah).

9. Āyatullāh al-ʿUẓmā Sayyid Ṣadiq Roḥānī

مستحب است گفتن اشهد ان امير المؤمنين عليا ولي الله يا اشهد ان عليا اميرالمؤمنين وولي الله در اذان و اقامه، بعد از اشهد ان محمدا رسول الله، بلكه چون در اين ازمنه اين جمله جزء شعائر مذهب تشيع می باشد و بعضی از فقهاء احتمال وجوب آن را داده اند، ترك نشود.

Ruling 955: It is recommended (*mustahab*) to say the phrase "أَشْهَدُ أَنَّ أَمِيرَ الْمُؤْمِنِينَ عَلِيّاً وَلِيُّ اللهِ" or to say "أَشْهَدُ أَنَّ عَلِيّاً أَمِيرَ الْمُؤْمِنِينَ وَلِيُّ اللهِ" in the *adhān* and *iqāmah* after: 'I bear witness that Muhammad is the Messenger of Allah' - "أَشْهَدُ أَنَّ مُحَمَّداً رَسُولُ اللهِ" – rather, in this era, as this phrase has become a part of the slogans of the Shīʿa and some of the scholars have stated that perhaps it is an obligation to be said, thus it must not be neglected.

10. Āyatullāh al-ʿUẓmā Sayyid ʿAlī Ḥusaynī Sīstānī

مسأله ۱۰۹۴. عبارت‌های «أَشْهَدُ أَنَّ عَلیّاً وَلِیُّ اللهِ» یا «أَشْهَدُ أنَّ عَلیّاً أمیرُ الْمُؤْمِنِینَ» یا «أَشْهَدُ أنَّ عَلیّاً أمیرُ الْمُؤْمِنِینَ وَوَلیُّ اللهِ» یا «أَشْهَدُ أنَّ عَلیّاً أمیرَ الْمُؤْمِنِینَ وَلیُّ اللهِ» جزء اذان و اقامه نیست هرچند شهادت و گواهی به ولایت و إمارت (امیر المؤمنین بودن) حضرت علی بن ابی طالب(علیهما السلام) به خودی خود مستحب است و کامل کننده شهادت به رسالت رسول اکرم(صلی الله علیه و آله) می‌باشد بنابر این خوب است بدون قصد جزئیت، بعد از «أَشْهَدُ أنَّ مُحَمَّداً رَسُوْلُ اللهِ» به نیّت قربت گفته شود.

Ruling 1094: The phrases - "أَشْهَدُ أَنَّ عَلِيّاً وَلِيُّ اللهِ" – "I bear witness that indeed ʿAlī is the *walī* of Allah"; or "أَشْهَدُ أنَّ عَليّاً أميرُ الْمُؤْمِنِينَ" – "I bear witness that indeed ʿAlī is the Commander of the Faithful'; or "أَشْهَدُ أنَّ عَليّاً أميرُ الْمُؤْمِنِينَ وَوَليُّ اللهِ" – "I bear witness that indeed ʿAlī is the Commander of the Faithful and the *walī* of Allah"; or "أَشْهَدُ أنَّ عَليّاً أميرَ الْمُؤْمِنِينَ وَليُّ اللهِ" – "I bear witness that indeed ʿAlī, the Commander of the Faithful, is the *walī* of Allah' – are not a part of the *adhān* and *iqāmah*, although bearing witness and testimony to the *wilāyah* and *imāmah* (being the Commander of the Faithful) of ʿAlī b. Abī Ṭālib ﷺ is, in and of itself a recommended (*mustaḥab*) action and actually completes the bearing witness and testimony to the messengership (*risālah*) of the Noble Prophet ﷺ and therefore it is advantageous that – without considering it as being a part [of the *adhān* and *iqāmah*], after saying "أَشْهَدُ أنَّ مُحَمَّداً رَسُوْلُ اللهِ", it is said with the intention of seeking closeness to Allah.

11. Āyatullāh al-ʿUẓmā Sayyid Muḥammad Ḥusaynī Shahrūdī

أَشْهَدُ أَنَّ عَلِيّاً وَلِيُّ اللّه جزء اذان و اقامه نیست. ولی خوبست بعد از أَشْهَدُ أَنَّ مُحَمَّداً رَسُولُ اللّهِ، به قصد قربت گفته شود.

Ruling 928: The phrase - 'I bear witness that indeed ʿAlī is the *walī* of Allah' - "أَشْهَدُ أَنَّ عَلِيّاً وَلِيُّ اللهِ" is not a part of the *adhān* and *iqāmah,* however it is good that it is said after: 'I bear witness that Muhammad is the Messenger of Allah' - "أَشْهَدُ أَنَّ مُحَمَّداً رَسُولُ اللهِ" with the intention of seeking nearness [to Allah].

12. Āyatullāh al-ʿUẓmā Shaykh Nāṣir Makārim Shīrāzī

«اَشْهَدُ أَنَّ عَلِيّاً وَلِيُّ اللّهِ» (یعنی گواهی می دهم که علی ولیّ خدا بر همه خلق است) جزء اذان و اقامه نیست، ولی خوب است بعد از «اَشْهَدُ أَنَّ مُحَمَّداً رَسُولُ اللّهِ» به قصد تبرّک گفته شود، لکن به صورتی که معلوم شود جزء آن نیست.

Ruling 843: The phrase - 'I bear witness that indeed ʿAlī is the *walī* of Allah' - "أَشْهَدُ أَنَّ عَلِيّاً وَلِيُّ اللهِ" (meaning that I bear witness that Ali is the *wali* of Allah over all of His creations) is not a part of the *adhān* or *iqāmah,* however it is good to say it after: 'I bear witness that Muhammad is the Messenger of Allah' - "أَشْهَدُ أَنَّ مُحَمَّداً رَسُولُ اللهِ" with the intention of seeking nearness [to Allah] – however [this is recited with this intention] knowing that it is not a part of them [the *adhān* or *iqāmah*].

13. Āyatullāh al-ʿUẓmā Sayyid Ṣādiq Shīrāzī

« أشْهَدُ أنَّ عَلِياً وَلِیُّ اللّه » جزو اذان و اقامه است. و در بعضی از روایات به آن اشاره شده است.

Ruling 1000: The phrase - 'I bear witness that indeed ʿAlī is the *walī* of Allah' - "أَشْهَدُ أَنَّ عَلِيّاً وَلِيُّ اللهِ" is a part of the *adhān* and *iqāmah* and this has been referred to in some of the narrations (*ḥadīth*).

جواب: شهادت ثالثه جزء اذان و اقامه است به این معنی که بدون آن اذان و اقامه ناقص است.

Answer 161: The third testimony [to the mastership of ʿAlī] is a part of the *adhān* and *iqāmah* meaning that without it, the *adhān* and *iqāmah* are incomplete.

14. Āyatullāh al-ʿUẓmā Shaykh Jaʿfar Subḥānī

أَشْهَدُ أَنَّ عَلِيّاً وَلِیُّ اللّه جزو اذان و اقامه نیست ولی خوب است بعد از أَشْهَدُ أَنَّ مُحَمَّداً رَسُولُ اللّهِ، به قصد قربت مطلقه و زینت اذان و اقامه گفته شود.

Ruling 775: The phrase - 'I bear witness that indeed ʿAlī is the *walī* of Allah' - "أَشْهَدُ أَنَّ عَلِيّاً وَلِيُّ اللهِ" is not a part of the *adhān* and *iqāmah*, however it is good that it is said after: 'I bear witness that Muhammad is the Messenger of Allah' - "أَشْهَدُ أَنَّ مُحَمَّداً رَسُولُ اللهِ" with the intention of seeking nearness [to Allah] and as a means of beautification of the *adhān* and *iqāmah*.

15. Āyatullāh al-ʿUẓmā Shaykh Mujtabā Ṭehrānī

وَ اَشْهَدُ اَنَّ عَلِيّا وَلِيُّ اللّه جزء اذان و اقامه نيست؛ ولى خوبست بعد از اشهد ان محمدا رسول اللّه، به قصد قربت گفته شود.

Ruling 919: The phrase - 'I bear witness that indeed ʿAlī is the *walī* of Allah' - "أَشْهَدُ أَنَّ عَلِيّاً وَلِيُّ اللهِ" is not a part of the *adhān* and *iqāmah,* however it is good that it is said after: 'I bear witness that Muhammad is the Messenger of Allah' - "أَشْهَدُ أَنَّ مُحَمَّداً رَسُولُ اللهِ" with the intention of seeking nearness [to Allah].

16. Āyatullāh al-ʿUẓmā Sayyid Shubayrī Zanjānī

«اشهد ان عليا ولي الله» جز اذان و اقامه نيست ؛ البته ولايت اميرالمؤمنين و ائمه معصومين عليهم السلام از اركان ايمان است و اسلام بدون آن، ظاهري بيش نيست و قالبي از معنا تهي است و خوب است كه پس از اشهد ان محمداً رسول الله به قصد تيمن و تبرك، شهادت به ولايت و امامت بلافصل حضرت اميرالمؤمنين و ساير معصومين عليهم السلام به گونه اى كه عرفا از اجزاى اذان و اقامه به حساب نيايد ذكر گردد.

[The phrase], 'I bear witness that indeed ʿAlī is the *walī* of Allah' is not a part of the *adhān* and *iqāmah*, however the *wilāyah* of the Commander of the Faithful and the infallible Imams, peace be upon all of them, is a pillar of true faith and without this [*wilāyah*], Islam is nothing more than an superficial submission [to Allah] and format of the meaning of it is empty, and therefore it is suitable that once a person says, "أَشْهَدُ أَنَّ مُحَمَّداً رَسُولُ اللهِ", that with the intention of seeking Divine benedictions and blessings, that one then bears witness to the *wilāyah,* and immediate *Imamah* [after the demise of the Noble Prophet ﷺ] of the Commander of the Faithful [ʿAlī (ʿa)] and the other infallibles, peace be upon all of them, in such a way that it is not considered as being a part of the *adhān* and *iqāmah* by those in the Islamic society.

17. Late Āyatullāh al-ʿUẓmā Muḥammad Taqī Behjat

بعید نیست مستحب بودن اقرار به ولایت امیرالمؤمنین علی بن ابیطالب علیه السلام در اذان مستحبی، در صورتی که به نیّت مطلوب بودن گفته شود ، به عبارات مختلفی که در « نهایه » و « فقیه » و « احتجاج » نقل شده است که « اَنَّ عَلِیّا وَلِیُّ اللّه » و یا « عَلِیٌّ اَمیرُ الْمُؤمِنین » و یا به عبارت « اَشْهَدُ اَنَّ عَلِیّا وَلِیُّ اللّه » باشد ، و اما اقرار به ولایت اگر چه در غیر اذان باشد خوب است ، پس احتیاج به دلیل مخصوص ندارد؛ و کاملترین عبارتی که در اینجا گفته می شود آن است که اقرار به خلیفه بودن یا وصی بودن حضرت امیرالمؤمنین علیه السلام و ائمه طاهرین علیهم السلام در آن باشد.

Ruling 36 on the *adhān* and *iqāmah*: It is not improbable that it is recommended (*mustaḥab*) to testify to the *wilāyah* of the Commander of the Faithful Ali b. Abi Talib, peace be upon him, in the recommended *adhān* with the intention that this act is a virtuous action; in various statements seen in [the books] *Nihāyah*, *Faqīh* and *Iḥtijāj* it has been related that the phrase – 'Indeed ʿAlī is the walī of Allah' - "أَنَّ عَلِيّاً وَلِيُّ اللهِ" or 'ʿAlī is the Commander of the Faithful' - "عَلِيٌّ أَمِيرُ الْمُؤْمِنِينَ" or in the wordings of - 'I bear witness that indeed ʿAlī is the *walī* of Allah' - "أَشْهَدُ أَنَّ عَلِيّاً وَلِيُّ اللهِ". However, as for testifying to the *wilāyah* in other than the *adhān*, then this is something which is good to do and thus, there is no need for proofs for this and the most complete of phrases which can be stated here (in the *adhān* or *iqāmah*) is that the Commander of the Faithful, peace be upon him and the

A'immah, peace be upon all of them, are the *khalīfah* or *waṣī* [of the Prophet].

18. Late Āyatullāh al-ʿUẓmā Sayyid Muḥammad Burujerdī

«اَشْهَدُ اَنَّ عَلِياً وَلِى اللهِ» جزء اذان و اقامه نيست، ولى خوب است بعد از «اَشْهَدُ اَنَّ مُحَمَّداً رسُولُ اللهِ» به قصد قربت گفته شود.

Ruling 928: The phrase - 'I bear witness that indeed ʿAlī is the *walī* of Allah' - "أَشْهَدُ أَنَّ عَلِيّاً وَلِيُّ اللهِ" is not a part of the *adhān* and *iqāmah,* however it is good that it is said after: 'I bear witness that Muhammad is the Messenger of Allah' - "أَشْهَدُ أَنَّ مُحَمَّداً رَسُولُ اللهِ" with the intention of seeking nearness [to Allah].

19. Late Āyatullāh al-ʿUẓmā Shaykh Luṭfullāh Ṣāfī Gulpāygānī

«أَشْهَدُ أَنَّ عَلِيّاً وَلِيُّ الله» جزو اذان و اقامه نيست، ولي خوب است بعد از «أَشْهَدُ أَنَّ مُحَمَّداً رَسوُلُ الله»، به قصد قربت گفته شود.

Ruling 928: The phrase - 'I bear witness that indeed ʿAlī is the *walī* of Allah' - "أَشْهَدُ أَنَّ عَلِيّاً وَلِيُّ اللهِ" is not a part of the *adhān* or *iqāmah,* however it is good that it is said after: 'I bear witness that Muhammad is the Messenger of Allah' - "أَشْهَدُ أَنَّ مُحَمَّداً رَسُولُ اللهِ" with the intention of seeking nearness [to Allah].

20. Late Āyatullāh al-ʿUẓmā Sayyid Ruḥullāh Khomeinī

"اشهد ان عليا ولى الله" جزو اذان و اقامه نيست، ولى خوب است بعداز "اشهد ان محمدا رسول الله" به قصد قربت گفته شود.

Ruling 919: The phrase - 'I bear witness that indeed ʿAlī is the walī of Allah' - "أَشْهَدُ أَنَّ عَلِيّاً وَلِيُّ اللهِ" is not a part of the *adhān* or *iqāmah,* however it is good to say it after saying: 'I bear witness that Muhammad is the Messenger of Allah' - "أَشْهَدُ أَنَّ مُحَمَّداً رَسُولُ اللهِ" with the intention of seeking nearness [to Allah].

21. Late Āyatullāh al-ʿUẓmā Shaykh Fādhil Lankarānī

اَشْهَدُ اَنَّ عَلياًّ وَلِىُّ اللهِ جزو اذان و اقامه نيست ولى خوب است بعد از اَشْهَدُ اَنَّ مُحَمَّداً رسُولُ اللهِ به قصد قربت گفته شود

Page 156 of his Islamic Rulings: The phrase - 'I bear witness that indeed ʿAlī is the *walī* of Allah' - "أَشْهَدُ أَنَّ عَلِيّاً وَلِيُّ اللهِ" is not a part of the *adhān* or *iqāmah,* however it is good that it is said after saying: 'I bear witness that Muhammad is the Messenger of Allah' - "أَشْهَدُ أَنَّ مُحَمَّداً رَسُولُ اللهِ" with the intention of seeking nearness [to Allah].

22. Late Āyatullāh al-ʿUẓmā Sayyid Muḥammad Shīrāzī

(أَشْهَدُ أَنَّ عَلِياً وَلِيُّ الله) جزو اذان و اقامه است. و در روایاتی به آن اشاره شده که در (الفقه) بيان نموده ایم.

Ruling 1000: The phrase - 'I bear witness that indeed ʿAlī is the *walī* of Allah' - "أَشْهَدُ أَنَّ عَلِيّاً وَلِيُّ اللهِ" is a part of the *adhān* and *iqāmah* and in some of the narrations (*ḥadīth*) this has been mentioned – and we have mentioned this (in our book *al-Fiqh*).

23. Late Āyatullāh al-ʿUẓmā Mīrzā Jawād Tabrizī

اشهد ان عليا ولى اللّه جزو اذان و اقامه نيست , ولى خوب است بعد از اشهد ان محمدا رسول اللّه به قصد قربت گفته شود.

Ruling 928: The phrase - 'I bear witness that indeed ʿAlī is the *walī* of Allah' - "أَشْهَدُ أَنَّ عَلِيّاً وَلِيُّ اللهِ" is not a part of the *adhān* or *iqāmah*, however it is good that it is said after: 'I bear witness that Muhammad is the Messenger of Allah' - "أَشْهَدُ أَنَّ مُحَمَّداً رَسُولُ اللهِ" with the intention of 'seeking nearness [to Allah]'

Appendix II

Islamic Laws of the *Adhān* and *Iqāmah*

The below is a translation extracted from the *Comprehensive Islamic Laws* (*Tawḍīḥ al-Masā'il Jāmi'*) manual of His Eminence, Āyatullāh al-'Uẓmā al-Ḥājj al-Sayyid 'Alī al-Ḥusaynī al-Sīstānī.

Ruling 1090: It is recommended (*mustaḥab*) for both the male and female that before each of the five daily prayers, they recite the *adhān* followed by the *iqāmah,* and there is added emphasis given for the recitation of the *adhān* and *iqāmah* for the morning (*ṣubḥ*) and evening (*maghrib*) prayers. In addition, reciting the *adhān* and *iqāmah* is something which has been further emphasized for the male (over the female), rather according to recommended precaution (*al-iḥtiyāṭ al-mustaḥab*), men should not abandon performing the *iqāmah.*

Ruling 1091: There is no religious basis for performing the *adhān* and *iqāmah* for the other obligatory prayers, other than the five daily prayers – such as *ṣalāt al-ayāt* and in addition, the other recommended prayers. However before one performs the *ṣalāt* of *'eīd al-fiṭr* and *al-aḍḥa,* if they are being performed in congregation, then it is recommended to say *as-ṣalāt* three times.

Ruling 1092: It is permissible to recite the *adhān* simply to inform the people that the time of *ṣalāt* is entering in and this is referred to as the '*adhān* of announcement'. It is necessary that the '*adhān* of announcement' is recited right when the time for the *ṣalāt* enters and that the person who gives this *adhān* is male, however there is no requirement to have the intention of 'seeking proximity to Allah' for this mode of *adhān.*

Method of Performing the *Adhān* and *Iqāmah*

Ruling 1093: The *adhān* has eighteen lines:

4 Times	أَللّٰهُ أَكْبَرُ
2 Times	أَشْهَدُ أَنْ لَا إِلٰهَ إِلَّا اللّٰهُ
2 Times	أَشْهَدُ أَنَّ مُحَمَّداً رَسُولُ اللّٰهِ
2 Times	حَيَّ عَلىٰ الصَّلَاةِ
2 Times	حَيَّ عَلىٰ الْفَلَاحِ
2 Times	حَيَّ عَلىٰ خَيْرِ الْعَمَلِ
2 Times	أَللّٰهُ أَكْبَرُ
2 Times	لَا إِلٰهَ إِلَّا اللّٰهُ

The *iqāmah* has seventeen lines:

2 Times	أَللّٰهُ أَكْبَرُ
2 Times	أَشْهَدُ أَنْ لَا إِلٰهَ إِلَّا اللّٰهُ
2 Times	أَشْهَدُ أَنَّ مُحَمَّداً رَسُولُ اللّٰهِ
2 Times	حَيَّ عَلىٰ الصَّلَاةِ
2 Times	حَيَّ عَلىٰ الْفَلَاحِ

2 Times	حَيَّ عَلىٰ خَيْرِ الْعَمَلِ
2 Times	قَدْ قَامَتِ الصَّلَاةِ
2 Times	أَللّٰهُ أَكْبَرُ
1 Time	لَا إِلٰهَ إِلَّا اللّٰهُ

Ruling 1094: The phrases - "أَشْهَدُ أَنَّ عَلِيّاً وَلِيُّ اللهِ" – "I bear witness that indeed ʿAlī is the *walī* of Allah"; or "أَشْهَدُ أَنَّ عَلِيّاً أميرُ الْمُؤْمِنِين" – "I bear witness that ʿAlī is the Commander of the Faithful'; or "أَشْهَدُ أَنَّ عَلِيّاً أميرُ الْمُؤْمِنِينَ وَوَلَىُّ اللهِ" – "I bear witness that indeed ʿAlī is the Commander of the Faithful and the *walī* of Allah"; or "أَشْهَدُ أَنَّ عَلِيّاً أميرَ الْمُؤْمِنِينَ وَلَىُّ اللهِ" – "I bear witness that indeed ʿAlī, the Commander of the Faithful, is the *walī* of Allah' – are not a part of the *adhān* and *iqāmah*, although bearing witness and testimony to the *wilāyah* and *imāmah* (being the Commander of the Faithful) of ʿAlī b. Abī Ṭālib ﷺ is in of itself a recommended (*mustaḥab*) action and actually completes the bearing witness and testimony to the messengership (*risālah*) of the Noble Prophet ﷺ, and therefore it is advantageous that – without considering it as being a part [of the *adhān* and *iqāmah*], after saying "أَشْهَدُ أَنَّ مُحَمَّداً رَسُوْلُ اللهِ" – "I bear witness that indeed Muḥammad is the Messenger of Allah", it is said with the intention of seeking closeness to Allah.

Ruling 1095: It is permissible for those who are travelling and also for those who are in a hurry to reduce the lines of the *adhān* and *iqāmah* to be recited one time each.

Translation of the lines of the *Adhān* and *Iqāmah*

Allah is greater [than what He is described as]	أَللّٰهُ أَكْبَرُ
I testify that there is no god but Allah	أَشْهَدُ أَنْ لَا إِلٰهَ إِلَّا اللّٰهُ
I testify that Muḥammad is the Messenger of Allah	أَشْهَدُ أَنَّ مُحَمَّداً رَسُولُ اللّٰهِ
I testify that ʿAlī is the vicegerent of Allah	أَشْهَدُ أَنَّ عَلِيّاً وَلِيُّ اللّٰهِ
Hasten to prayers	حَيَّ عَلَى الصَّلَاةِ
Hasten to prosperity	حَيَّ عَلَى الْفَلَاحِ
Hasten to the best of actions	حَيَّ عَلَى خَيْرِ الْعَمَلِ
Certainly, the prayer has been established	قَدْ قَامَتِ الصَّلَاةِ
There is no god but Allah	لَا إِلٰهَ إِلَّا اللّٰهُ

Conditions Regarding the *Adhān* and *Iqāmah*

Ruling 1096: The specifics in regards to the '*adhān* of announcement' was mentioned in the previous ruling (1092), however the *adhān* and *iqāmah* for the [daily] prayers also has conditions which we will go over in the following rulings.

Condition 1, 2 and 3: A person who performs the *adhān* and *iqāmah* must be sane, a *Shīʿa Ithnā-Asherī* (believer of the 12 Imams) and for a [congregational] prayer of men [or one in which men and women are present], the *adhān* and *iqāmah* must be recited by a male.

Ruling 1097: The only time that the *adhān* and *iqāmah* are correct by a person who performs them is when one is sane; a *Shīʿa Ithnā-Asherī,* and if the congregational prayer is of men [men only or if women are also present], then the *adhān* and *iqāmah* must be performed by a male.[32]

However, being *bāligh* (having reached the age of maturity) is not a condition for the *adhān* [to be valid]. Therefore, if a person hears the *adhān* being given by a child who is not *bāligh,* however the child is *mumayyiz*[33], or was told that such a child gave the *adhān,* or a non-*bāligh* child who is *mumayyiz* gave the *adhān* for a congregational prayer, then their *adhān* is sufficient, however according to obligatory precaution (*al-iḥtiyāt al-wājib*), one can not suffice with the *iqāmah* of a non-*bāligh* child who is *mumayyiz* [and not *bāligh*].[34]

---

[32] It is worth noting that if a woman who is present in a gathering with men who are all her *maḥram* performs the *adhān* and *iqāmah* for them for the congregational prayers, then according to obligatory precaution, this would not be sufficient [and one of the men must perform the *adhān* and *iqāmah*].

[33] Someone who is able to discern between right and wrong; a discerning minor. (Tr.)

[34] Explaining the issues relating to if the *adhān* and *iqāmah* of others is sufficient will be reviewed in the upcoming rulings.

It should also be noted that the *adhān* and *iqāmah* performed by a child who is non-*bāligh* and *mumayyiz* is not a problem for their own prayers and is sufficient [for them].

Condition 4, 5 & 6: The *adhān* and *iqāmah* must be performed with the intention of seeking proximity to Allah ﷻ and with full sincerity (*al-ikhlāṣ*), and in the event that there are multiple prayers being performed, then one needs to specify for which prayer the *adhān* and *iqāmah* are being recited.

Ruling 1097: All of the lines in the *adhān* and *iqāmah* performed for the *ṣalāt* must be done with the intention of seeking proximity to Allah ﷻ and with full sincerity (*al-ikhlāṣ*), and must also be recited in the correct Arabic. If the *adhān* and *iqāmah* are shared between multiple prayers, then it must be specified for which prayers the *adhān* and *iqāmah* are being performed. For example, a person who has the intention to perform the prayer for that particular day and also has missed prayers which need to be performed, must clearly specify (in the intention) that the *adhān* and *iqāmah* which he is reciting are for a specific *ṣalāt* [either the current prayers or the recompensed missed prayers]; or for example, a person who intends to perform multiple missed prayers must specify, when performing the *adhān* and *iqāmah* as to which missed prayer he is performing the *adhān* and *iqāmah* for.

Condition 7: Follow the Sequence of Lines

Ruling 1099: The *iqāmah* must be performed after the *adhān* and therefore, if a person deliberately, mistakenly or because of not knowing the rule, says the *iqāmah* before the *adhān*, then in order for him to ensure that he has acted according to this recommended action (of the *adhān* and *iqāmah*), it is necessary that one re-performs the *adhān* (and then follows it up with the *iqāmah*) afterwards.

Ruling 1100: It is incumbent to maintain order when reciting the lines of the *adhān* and *iqāmah,* and therefore if a person does not say the lines of the *adhān* and *iqāmah* in order, and for example says: "حَيَّ عَلَى الْفَلاحِ" – "Hasten to success" before "حَيَّ عَلَى الصَّلاةِ" – "Hasten to the prayers", then one must repeat the lines which were not said in order; unless the sequence of saying the lines is completely broken as in such a scenario, one must repeat the *adhān* and *iqāmah* from the beginning.

Condition 8: Maintain Succession of the Statements

Ruling 1101: There must not be a large time gap between the individual lines of the *adhān* and *iqāmah*, and if between the lines, a time gap larger than normal is retained which would break the flow of the *adhān* and *iqāmah* and the people would say that the person has not performed the *adhān* and *iqāmah*, then such an *adhān* and *iqāmah* are not sufficient [and they must be repeated].

Ruling 1102: An individual performing the *adhān* and *iqāmah* must not maintain a large gap of time between the two of these [the *adhān* and *iqāmah*] and if there is a large time gap between the two of them such that the *adhan* which was performed would not be considered (by the masses) as being the *adhān* for that specific *iqāmah*, then that *adhān* is not sufficient for that *ṣalāt*. However if the gap which is between the *adhān* and *iqāmah* is such as is mentioned in **Ruling 1120**, then this will not result in a breaking in the succession. In addition, if between the *adhān* and *iqāmah* and the *ṣalāt*, there is a gap such that the *adhān* and *iqāmah* performed are not considered [by the people] as being for that specific *ṣalāt*, then it is not sufficient [and they must be repeated].

Condition 9: Time for Ṣalāt Must have Set In

Ruling 1103: The *adhān* and *iqāmah* must be performed once the time for the prayers has arrived, and if intentionally or due to forgetfulness, they are performed before the time of the *ṣalāt*, then they are invalid; except in the case when the time of prayer sets in during a prayer and the prayer is ruled as being valid, as will be explained in **Rule 1418.**[35]

---

[35] **Ruling 1418:** If one of the religious ways stated in Ruling 894 proves to a person that the time for the prayers has started and they are engaged in prayer:

- **a.** If he finds out in the course of a prayer that he has miscalculated and it is still not time for prayer - even though he realized only moments after the time of the prayer had come in, his prayers are invalid.
- **b.** If he doubts in the course of the prayer that the time of prayers has arrived or shortly the time of prayers will start, then his prayers will be invalid.
- **c.** If he realizes during the course of the prayers that after he started the prayers, the time of the prayers began such that while in the course of his prayers, he realized that it was at that point that the actual time for the prayers started, then his prayers are correct.
- **d.** If there is certainty or confidence in the course of the prayers that the time of the prayers has arrived and then one doubts if whatever he has performed of the prayers was within the time or not, then the prayer is correct.
- **e.** If he realizes after completing the prayer that during the course of performing the prayers the time of the prayers began, then his prayers are correct.

Condition 10: Iqāmah Must be Performed Standing Up

Ruling 1104: In order for the *iqāmah* to be deemed as valid, as much as possible, the person performing it must be standing when one recites it; however as for standing while performing the *adhān*, this is recommended.

Condition 11: Iqāmah and the State of Purity

Ruling 1105: When a person is performing the *iqāmah*, they must be, according to obligatory precaution, in a state of purity either via a *ghusl*, *wuḍhū* or *tayammum* (whatever a person's responsibility is to perform). However as for the *adhān*, maintaining purity is only recommended [not an obligation].

Condition 12: Adhān and Iqāmah Must Not be "Sung"

Ruling 1106: If the *adhān* and *iqāmah* are recited in such a way that they are considered as being "sung", meaning that they are recited in such a way as is commonly done by singers who perform in gatherings of futility (clubs, concerts, parties, etc.), then this is impermissible (*ḥarām*), and if it is not done in a style of singing [but is also not recited in the appropriate style as has been commonly used for the *adhān* and *iqāmah*], then it is reprehensible (*makrūh*).

---

f. And lastly, if after the completion of the prayer, he doubts whether he performed the prayers on time or before their time set in, then while at the time of doubt, if the time of the prayers had arrived, then the prayers are correct.

Times when the Adhān is not Required

Ruling 1107: In all cases in which a worshipper performs two prayers that have a common time (such as the *ṣalāt* of *dhuhr* and *ʿaṣr* or the *ṣalāt* of *maghrib* and *ʿishā*),[36] if for the first prayer, the *adhān* is performed, then there is no need to perform it for the next prayer; whether performing the two prayers right after one another is better or not – for example, the performance of the prayers of *dhuhr* and *ʿaṣr* on the day of *ʿArafah* (the 9th day of the month of *Dhul Ḥijjah*); if this prayer is done during the recommended time of *dhuhr*, then it is recommended, even though one is not in the land of *ʿArafah*. Also the performance of the *maghrib* and *ʿishā* prayers on the day of *ʿeīd al-aḍḥā* at the prime time of the *ʿishā* prayer for a person who is present in the land known as *Mashʿar al-Ḥarām* [just outside of Mecca which is one of the places which the pilgrims are expected to be during the *ḥajj* pilgrimage].

If in the above cases, a person performs the two prayers 'together' [one immediately after the other] and then wants to say the *adhān* for the second prayer, then according to obligatory precaution, the *adhān* for the second prayer must be performed with the intention of *rajāʾ* [hope that it be accepted by Allah ﷻ] and must not be performed with the intent that this is something legitimized within the religious teachings. Rather, on the basis of obligatory precaution, the *adhān* for the second prayer, in the two cases mentioned above – that is on the day of *ʿArafah* and while in *Mashʿar al-Ḥarām* – with the conditions stated above –

---

[36] This is a reference to when the two prayers (*dhuhr* and *ʿaṣr* / *maghrib* and *ʿishā*) are performed back to back – without them being performed in their 'specific' timings.

must be performed without the intention that this is something legitimized in the Islamic rulings and must be done merely with the intention of *rajāʾ*.

It is worth noting that the abandonment of the *adhān* in these cases is conditional on the fact that there must be no large time gap between the two prayers, however adding a time gap between the two prayers to perform the recommend prayers (*nawāfil*) and other supplications (*taʿqibāt*) between the prayers is not harmful.

Times When the Adhān and Iqāmah are Not Required

Ruling 1108: If the *adhān* and *iqāmah* have been performed for a congregational prayer, then the person who is performing the prayers within that congregation is not required to perform the *adhān* and *iqāmah* again, even though he has not heard the *adhān* and *iqāmah* [which were originally given], and it does not matter whether the prayer of the congregation has already been established or is about to be held. Also, if they [the *adhān* and *iqāmah* were given close to the time of] the congregational prayer, then it does not matter whether the Imam enters the congregation or the followers have entered the congregation [and hear the *adhān* and *iqāmah* being offered]; however, in these cases, according to obligatory precaution, a worshipper must not perform the *adhān* and *iqāmah* for his prayers with the intention that it is a legislated act.[37]

[37] Unless a person who enters the congregation is the worshipper who is following in the prayers, and the *imam* of the congregation is someone whom one is not permitted to pray behind as in this scenario, the *adhān* and *iqāmah* which was performed by a person who is performing their prayers in that congregation, is not stopped [and thus, it should be performed].

Ruling 1109: If a person goes to a *masjid* to perform the prayers and sees that the congregational prayers are completed, then as long as the lines of the worshippers have not broken apart and the people have not dispersed, with the conditions appearing in the next ruling, one does not have to say the *adhān* and *iqāmah* for one's own individual prayers – meaning that it is not something which is considered as expressly recommended to do. But if one wants to say the *adhān*, then it is better to say it in a very low voice, and if one wants to start a new congregational prayer, then one must not recite the *adhān* and *iqāmah.*

Ruling 1110: In the case mentioned above, with six conditions, the *adhān* and *iqāmah* are abandoned:

First: The congregational prayer is performed in a ***masjid*** as this ruling does not apply to **non-*masājid*.**

Second: For that prayer [that has completed but the lines have not dispersed], the *adhān* and *iqāmah* should have been [previously] said.

Third: The congregational prayer was not deemed void. For example, if the *imam* of the congregation is not a righteous person and the worshippers praying behind him become aware of this, then the *adhān* and *iqāmah* [for the individual coming into the *masjid*] are not dropped.

Fourth: The person's prayers and the prayers of the congregation are in one place. Thus, if the congregational prayer is held inside of the *masjid* and the person wishes to, for example, perform the prayers on the roof of the *masjid*, then it is recommended that the *adhān* and *iqāmah* are performed again.

Fifth: The prayer of the congregation and the prayer of the individual are both performed within their time (*adāʾ*); so if the prayer of the congregation or the prayer of the individual or both of them is a prayer which was lapsed (and is being performed outside of its time), then the *adhān* and *iqāmah* are not dropped. However, it is unlikely that the worshipper who is performing his prayers on his own (and not within the congregation) would have his *adhān* dropped [and not required for him to perform], although the prayers which he is performing are those which he is doing to make up for a missed prayer.

Sixth: The time for his prayers and for the prayer of the congregation are the same, for example, both are performing the *dhuhr* prayers or the *ʿaṣr* prayers, or that the prayer of the congregation was the *dhuhr* prayer and the person's prayer was the *ʿaṣr* prayer or vice versaؼ but if the prayers of the congregation for the *ʿaṣr* prayers were being done at the end of their legislated time and the lines of that prayer of the congregation has not broken down and the individual wants to pray the *maghrib* prayers right when the time sets in and wants to perform the *adhān* for *maghrib* as well, then the *adhān* and *iqāmah* are not eliminated [and as such, they must be performed].

Ruling 1111: If an individual doubts in the third condition of the conditions of the preceding question — that is, he doubts[38] whether the prayers of the congregation are correct or not, then

[38] The meaning of a doubt in this portion, is not a doubt in the actual ruling; rather, it is in regards to the instance in which a person who because he does not know the specifics of the congregational prayer which has taken place, and so he has a doubt in regards to it being a valid prayer or not.

he must accept them as being valid, and consequently the *adhān* and *iqāmah* are not required to be performed. But if there is a doubt in one of the other five conditions, or if there is a doubt if the lines of the congregation have dispersed, based on what the common people would determine in regards to this, then the obligatory precaution is that the *adhān* and *iqāmah* are to be performed; but if the second prayer is performed in the congregation, then the *adhān* and *iqāmah* must be said with the intention of *rajā'*.

Issue 1112: Anyone who has heard the *adhān* and *iqāmah* recited by someone else, whether it was said 'for' him or not, if there is not much of a time distance between that *adhān* and *iqāmah* and the *ṣalāt* which one wants to read, and that individual had the intention to perform his prayers at the beginning of hearing the *adhān* and *iqāmah*, then one can suffice with that *adhān* and *iqāmah*. This ruling is a matter of doubt in regards to an instance for a congregational prayer in which only the *imam* of that congregation has heard the *adhān* or only the worshippers have heard that *adhān*. Also, if one does not hear a part of the *adhān* and *iqāmah*, then it is permissible to say the sentences which he did not hear and to suffice with such an *adhān* and *iqāmah* provided that the order of the lines of the *adhān* and *iqāmah* has been observed. Regarding hearing the *adhān* and *iqāmah* of another person, there is no difference between hearing (simply having the sounds in your audible range, but not really paying attention to it), and listening (actually listening to it and paying attention to it with the intention of listening).

Ruling 1113: If a man listens to the *adhān* and *iqāmah* delivered by a woman, and he has done so with the intention of deriving pleasure [from her voice], then he will have committed a sin and the *adhān* and *iqāmah* are not dropped from him; infact, according to obligatory precaution, one cannot merely suffice with listening to the *adhān* and *iqāmah* given by a woman even if it was done so without the intention of gaining pleasure [from hearing her voice]; and also – as already mentioned – according to obligatory precaution, one cannot suffice with the *adhān* and *iqāmah* given by a woman for a congregational prayer which is held with men present – even if those men are her relatives (*mahārim*).

Other Rulings of the *Adhān* and *Iqāmah*

Ruling 1114: If before performing the *iqāmah*, a person doubts whether or not one recited the *adhān*, then one should first perform the *adhān*; however if one is busy in the *iqāmah* and then doubts whether or not one pronounced the *adhān*, then it is not necessary to go back and recite the *adhān*.

Ruling 1115: If a person in the middle of the *adhān* and *iqāmah*, before one is about to say a line from it, doubts if one recited the preceding line or not, then that person must say that section which is doubted about; however if during the time of saying that portion of the *adhān* and *iqāmah*, one doubts about something which was before it and whether it was recited or not, then it is not necessary to say it.

Recommended Actions of the *Adhān* and *Iqāmah*

The great jurists, may Allah be pleased with all of them, have mentioned some recommended actions for the *adhān* and *iqāmah* – some of which we mention in the upcoming rulings.

Ruling 1116: It is recommended that a person who has been appointed to declare the *adhān* is just (*'ādil*) and knows the timings [of the prayer], and that he has a loud voice, and that he pronounces the *adhān* while standing at an elevated place.

Ruling 1117: It is recommended for one who is hearing another person recite the *adhān* – whether it is the '*adhān* of announcing' or the *adhān* signaling the congregational prayer — that every part he hears, he repeats it in a low voice, and this is referred to as 'emulating the *adhān' (ḥikāyah al-adhān).* Also, the 'emulating of the *iqāmah'* (*ḥikāyah al-iqāmah*) for a person who is performing his prayers in congregation is also something which is recommended. However, it is desirable that the listener says the following supplication when he hears "قَدْ قَامَتِ الصَّلَاة":

أَللَّهُمَّ أَقِمْهَا وَأَدِمْهَا وَاجْعَلْنِي مِنْ خَيْرِ صَالِحِي أَهْلِهَا

> O Allah! I have established it [the *ṣalāt*] and I have continued it, so make me one of the good righteous ones among it.

As for 'emulating the *adhān* and *iqāmah'* for a person who intends to perform the *ṣalāt* on their own (and not in congregation), is something not free of doubt, however doing so with the intention of *rajā'* is not a problem.

Ruling 1118: It is recommended that a person should stand facing the *qiblah* at the time of pronouncing the *adhān*; be with *wuḍhū* or *ghusl*; place his two thumbs on the ears; pronounces the *adhān* in a loud voice; stretches out the sentences; maintain a brief pause between the individual lines of the *adhān*; and not talk between the lines of the *adhān*.

Ruling 1119: It is recommended that the body be still at the time of reciting the *iqāmah,* and that it should be spoken with a slightly quieter voice than what was used for the *adhān* and that the lines of it are recited separate from one another (with slight gaps), however not the same distance between the separation of the sentences which was done in the *adhān.*

Ruling 1120: It is recommended to keep a time gap between the recitation of the *adhān* and *iqāmah* in the amount of time needed to take one step, or the time needed to sit down for a brief period, or prostrate, or say one *dhikr* such as "سُبْحَانَ اللّهِ" – "*Subḥanāllah*", or the recitation of a supplication, or remaining silent, or to say a word, or to perform a two *rakʿat* prayer – however it is not recommended to speak between the *adhān* and *iqāmah* of the *fajr* prayer.

Ruling 1121: It is not unlikely [meaning: it is possible] that reciting the *adhān* and *iqāmah* for women in their own *ṣalāt* could be an independent recommended action, and therefore by women not reciting the *adhān* and *iqāmah* for their own *ṣalāt* would not lead to their prayers not reaching to the highest stages of perfection; just like when it comes to the *adhān,* it is permissible for women to suffice with merely saying the *takbīr* [أَللّهُ أَكْبَر] and the *shahadatayn* [أَشْهَدُ أَنْ لاَ إِلَهَ إِلَّا اللّهُ وَأَنَّ مُحَمَّداً عَبْدُهُ وَرَسُوْلُهُ]. Rather, they can suffice with merely saying the *shahadatayn* and in addition, it is permissible for women to simply say the following in the *iqāmah*:

أَللّهُ أَكْبَر، أَشْهَدُ أَنْ لاَ إِلَهَ إِلَّا اللّهُ وَأَنَّ مُحَمَّداً عَبْدُهُ وَرَسُوْلُهُ

even though it is better that they say the *adhān* and *iqāmah* in the complete forms.

Appendix III

Supplications to Recite While the Adhān is Being Recited

1. Imam al-Ṣādiq ﷺ advised the faithful that when the *adhān* for the *fajr* and *maghrib* prayers are going on, that the following supplication should be recited, and if a person was to die at this time, then one will be considered as being amongst those who enacted repentance to Allah ﷻ:

أَللّٰهُمَّ إِنِّى أَسْأَلُکَ بِإِقْبَالِ لَيْلَتِکَ وَ إِدْبَارِ نَهَارِکَ وَ حُضُورِ
صَلَوَاتِکَ وَ أَصْوَاتِ دُعَائِکَ وَ تَسْبِيحِ مَلَائِکَتِکَ أَنْ تُصَلِّىَ عَلَىٰ
مُحَمَّدٍ وَ آلِ مُحَمَّد وَ أَنْ تَتُوبَ عَلَىَّ إِنَّکَ أَنْتَ التَّوَّابُ الرَّحِيم

O Allah! I ask You alone at the time when Your night arrives and Your day begins and when the presence of Your prayers comes, and the 'voice' of Your supplication and the glorification enacted by Your angels, that You send Your prayers upon Muḥammad and the family of Muḥammad and that You turn towards me as indeed You are the Oft-Turning [towards Your sinful creations], the Most-Merciful.[39]

2. When the *muaddhin* says:

أَشْهَدُ أَنْ لَا إِلٰهَ إِلَّا اللّٰهُ وَ أَشْهَدُ أَنَّ مُحَمَّداً رَسُولُ اللّٰهِ

[39] Sayyid Ibn Ṭāwūs, Raḍhī al-Dīn ʿAlī, *Falāḥ al-Sāʾīl wa Najāḥ al-Masāʾil*, p. 227.

I bear witness that there is no god other than Allah; and I bear witness that Muḥammad is the Messenger of Allah.

If at that time, a person listening to the *adhān* was to say the following supplication with full conviction and belief deep down inside of oneself, then Allah will forgive as many sins as there are people who denied Him and who accepted Him.[40]

أَنَا أَشْهَدُ أَنْ لَا إِلٰهَ إِلَّا اللّٰهَ وَ أَشْهَدُ أَنَّ مُحَمَّداً رَسُولُ اللّٰهِ وَ أَكْتَفِي بِهِمَا عَمَّنْ أَبىٰ وَ جَحَدَ وَ أُعِينُ بِهِمَا مَنْ أَقَرَّ وَ شَهِدَ

> I bear witness that indeed there is no god except for Allah and I bear witness that indeed Muḥammad is the Messenger of Allah and I suffice myself with both of them from all of those who are stubborn [against them] and dispute [with them] and I support all of those who also bear witness and testify to these two.

3. When the *muaddhin* says: 'أَشْهَدُ أَنَّ مُحَمَّداً رَسُولُ اللّٰهِ', the person listening to the *adhān* should recite the following:

صَلَّى اللّٰهُ عَلَيْهِ وَ آلِهِ الطَّاهِرِينَ أَللّٰهُمَّ اجْعَلْ عَمَلِي بِرّاً وَ مَوَدَّةَ آلِ مُحَمَّدٍ فِي قَلْبِي مُسْتَقَرّاً وَ أَدِرَّ عَلَيَّ الرِّزْقَ دَارّاً

Prayers of Allah be upon him and upon his purified family. O Allah! Allow my [good] deeds to be dutiful; and allow the deep love for the family of Muḥammad to be entrenched in my heart and allow sustenance to flow abundantly upon me.

In addition, when the *muaddhin* says "حَيَّ عَلَى الصَّلَاةِ" and "حَيَّ عَلَى الْفَلَاحِ", a person listening to the *adhān* should say the following:

---

[40] Kulaynī, Muḥammad b. Yaʿqūb, *al-Kāfī*, v. 3, p. 307.

لَا حَوْلَ وَ لَا قُوَّةَ إِلَّا بِاللهِ الْعَلِيِّ الْعَظِيمِ

There is no power and no strength save with Allah, the Most High, the Grand.[41]

At the Completion of the Adhān

The narrator of the following *ḥadīth* states that:

At the time of sunset, I was with Imam al-Ṣādiq ﵇ and I saw that after performing the *adhān*, the Imam sat down and was busy in reciting a supplication, in a way which I have never seen before. I remained quiet until the Imam completed his *ṣalāt* and then said to him: 'O my master! I heard a supplication from you the likes of which I have never heard ever before.'

The Imam replied: 'This is the supplication of the Commander of the Faithful ﵇ which he recited on the night when he slept in the bed of the Prophet ﷺ' and it is as follows:

يَا مَنْ لَيْسَ مَعَهُ رَبٌّ يُدْعَىٰ يَا مَنْ لَيْسَ فَوْقَهُ خَالِقٌ يُخْشَىٰ يَا مَنْ لَيْسَ دُونَهُ إِلٰهٌ يُتَّقَىٰ يَا مَنْ لَيْسَ لَهُ وَزِيرٌ يُغْشَىٰ يَا مَنْ لَيْسَ لَهُ بَوَّابٌ يُنَادَىٰ يَا مَنْ لَا يَزْدَادُ عَلَىٰ كَثْرَةِ السُّوَالِ إِلَّا كَرَماً وَ جُوداً يَا مَنْ لَا يَزْدَادُ عَلَىٰ عِظَمِ الْجُرْمِ إِلَّا رَحْمَةً وَ عَفْواً صَلِّ عَلَىٰ مُحَمَّدٍ وَ آلِ مُحَمَّدٍ وَ افْعَلْ بِی مَا أَنْتَ أَهْلُهُ فَإِنَّکَ أَهْلُ التَّقْوىٰ وَ أَهْلُ الْمَغْفِرَةِ وَ أَنْتَ أَهْلُ الْجُودِ وَ الْخَيْرِ وَ الْكَرَمِ

[41] Ṭabrisī, Ḥasan b. Faḍhl, *Makārim al-Akhlāq*, p. 298, Qum, Sharīf Raḍhī Publishers, 4th Printing, 1412 AH.

O the One whom there is no lord with Him [in His Lordship] that He would need to call upon! O the One above whom there is no creation whom He is scared of! O the One for whom there is no god other than Him to rely upon. O the One whom there is no minister that hides things from Him! O the One whom there is no concierge to be called upon! O the One who is not increased by the multitude of requests asked [from Him] – except [that He increases in His] nobility and generosity! O the One who is not increased in the grandeur of the sins [which His servants perform] except [in Him showing His creations] mercy and forgiveness! Send Your prayers upon Muḥammad and the family of Muḥammad and deal with me in the way which You are deserving of [treating Your servants], as indeed You are the most deserving of piety, and You are the most deserving of [granting] forgiveness, and You are the most deserving of generosity, goodness and nobility.[42]

[42] *Falāḥ al-Sā'il wa Najāḥ al-Masā'il*, p. 228.

Other Publications Available[43]

1. *40 Aḥādīth: Completion of Islam – Ghadīr* written by Mahmud Sharifi and translated by Saleem Bhimji[3]
2. 40 Aḥādīth: Qur᾿an written by Sayyid Majid Adili and translated by Arifa Hudda and Saleem Bhimji[3 and 4]
3. 40 Aḥādīth: The Saviour of Humanity – the 12th Imam in the Eyes of the Ahl al-Bayt written by Nasir Karimi and translated by Saleem Bhimji[3]
4. *40 Aḥādīth: The Spiritual Journey – Ḥajj* written by Mahmud Mahdipur and translated by Saleem Bhimji[3]
5. A Biography of the Marjaʿ Taqlid of the Shiʿa World: Ayatullah al-Uzma Sayyid ʿAli al-Ḥusayni al-Sistani translated by Saleem Bhimji[5]
6. *A Code of Ethics for Muslim Men and Women* written by Sayyid Masʿud Maʿsumi and translated by Arifa Hudda and Saleem Bhimji[1]

---

[43] The following is a list of books which are available from the Islamic Publishing House and publishers which it has worked with. A note on the pubishers noted above:

1 = *Islamic Humanitarian Service* (Canada) – www.al-haqq.com
2 = *Al-Fath Al-Mubin Publications* (Canada) – www.al-mubin.org
3 = *World Federation of KSIMC* (UK) – www.world-federation.org
4 = *Islamic Publishing House* (Canada) – www.iph.org
5 = Various publishers
6 = Not available in print [either an eBook] or out of print
7 = *Jaffari Propagation Centre* (India) – www.jpconline.org

Most of the above books and hundreds of other articles can be read for free at **www.al-mubin.org** or **www.al-islam.org**

7. *A Mother's Prayer* compiled and translated by Saleem Bhimji and Arifa Hudda[1 and 2]
8. A Star Amongst the Stars: Biography of Jābir ibn ʿAbdullāh al-Anṣārī by Shaykh Jaffer Ladak[4]
9. A Summary of the Rulings of Ṣalātul Jamāʿat according to the edicts of Ayatullah al-Uzma Sayyid ʿAli al-Ḥusayni al-Sistani compiled and translated by Saleem Bhimji[1]
10. *Alif, Baa, Taa of Kerbala* written by Saleem Bhimji and Arifa Hudda[4]
11. *Arbāʿīn of Imam Ḥusayn* compiled and translated by Saleem Bhimji[6]
12. Contentious issues in Islamc History – Umar ibn al-Khaṭṭāb witten by Saeed Dawari and translated by Saleem Bhimji[6]
13. *Deficient? A Review of Sermon 80 from Nahj al-Balāgha* by Ayatullah al-Uzma Shaykh Nasir Makarim Shirazi and translated by Saleem Bhimji[6]
14. *Ethical Discourses – Volume 1* written by Ayatullah al-Uzma Shaykh Nasir Makarim Shirazi and translated by Saleem Bhimji[(not printed)]
15. *Ethical Discourses – Volume 2* written by Ayatullah al-Uzma Shaykh Nasir Makarim Shirazi and translated by Saleem Bhimji[(not printed)]
16. *Exegesis of the 29th Juz of the Qur'ān – a Translation of Tafsīr-i Nemuneh* by Ayatullah al-Uzma Shaykh Nasir Makarim Shirazi and translated by Saleem Bhimji[1 and 4]

17. *Foundations of Islamic Unity* – an English translation of *Al-Fuṣūl Al-Muhimmah Fī Ta'līf al-Ummah* written by ʿAbd al-Ḥusayn Sharaf al-Dīn al-Mūsawī al-ʿĀmilī and translated by Batool Ispahany

18. *Fountain of Paradise – Fāṭima az-Zahrā' in the Noble Quran* written by Ayatullah al-Uzma Shaykh Nasir Makarim Shirazi compiled and translated by Saleem Bhimji[4, 5 and 7]

19. *God and god of science* by Syed Hasan Raza Jafri[4]

20. *Guiding the Youth of the New Generation* written by Ayatullah Shaykh Murtadha Mutahhari and translated by Saleem Bhimji[2 and 3]

21. *History Behind Masjid Jamkarān* along with Selected Supplications to the 12th Imam and translated by Saleem Bhimji[1]

22. *House of Sorrows* written by Shaykh ʿAbbas al-Qummi and translated by Aejaz ʿAlī Turab Ḥusayn Hussayni[4]

23. Inspirational Insights by Mohammed Khaku[4]

24. *Introduction to Islam* written by Saleem Bhimji[1]

25. *Introduction to the Science of Tafsīr of the Quran* written by Shaykh Jaʿfar Subhani and translated by Saleem Bhimji[3]

26. *Islam and Religious Pluralism* by Ayatullah Shaykh Murtadha Mutahhari and translated by Sayyid Sulayman ʿAlī Hasan[3]

27. *Islamic Edicts on Family Planning* by the UNFPA with the Ministry of Health of the Islamic Republic of Iran and translated by Saleem Bhimji[5]

28. *Istikhāra: Seeking the Best from Allah* written by Muḥammad Baqir Hayderi and translated by Saleem Bhimji[1]

29. *Journey to Eternity – A Handbook of Supplications for the Soul* compiled and translated by Saleem Bhimji and Arifa Hudda[4 and 7]

30. *Khums: The Islamic Tax* written by Ayatullah al-Uzma Shaykh Nasir Makarim Shirazi and translated by Saleem Bhimji[(not printed)]

31. *Love and Hate for Allah's Sake* by Mujtaba Saburi translated by Saleem Bhimji[4, 5 and 7]

32. *Love for the Family* compiled and translated by Yasin T. Al-Jibouri, Saleem Bhimji and others[4, 5 and 7]

33. Manifestation of the Divine Light – A Glimpse into the Ziyārah of Fāṭimah az-Zahrā' by Shaykh ʿAli Saʿadat Parwar translated by Saleem Bhimji[4]

34. *Meʿrāj: The Night Ascension* written by Mullah Muḥammad Faydh al-Kashani and translated by Saleem Bhimji[1]

35. Message of the Quran a translation of Payām-e-Quran – Volume 1 – A Thematic Exegesis of the Noble Quran written by Ayatullah al-Uzma Shaykh Nasir Makarim Shirazi and translated by Saleem Bhimji[3]

36. *Method of Ṣalāt* written by Muḥammad Qadhi and translated by Saleem Bhimji[5]

37. *Moral Management* written by ʿAbbas Rahimi and translated by Saleem Bhimji[4 and 7]

38. *Morals of the Masumeen* written by Arifa Hudda[4]

39. *On the Shore of Contemplation - Authority of the Jurist* – Compiled by the office of Ayatullah Ja'far Subhani and translated by Saleem Bhimji[4]

40. *Prayers of the Final Prophet – A collection of supplications of Prophet Muḥammad* written by ʿAllamah Sayyid Muḥammad Ḥusayn Taba'taba'i and translated by Tahir Ridha-Jaffer[4 and 7]

41. *Ramaḍhān Reflections* compiled by A Group of Muslim Scholars and translated by Saleem Bhimji[4 and 7]

42. Rules Relating to the Deceased: Condensed Version according to the edicts of Ayatullah al-Uzma Sayyid ʿAli al-Ḥusayni al-Sistani translated by Saleem Bhimji[1]

43. Rules Relating to the Deceased: Philosophy and Ahkam according to the edicts of Ayatullah al-Uzma Sayyid ʿAli al-Ḥusayni al-Sistani and translated by Saleem Bhimji[1]

44. *Salat al-Ayat* written by Saleem Bhimji[1 and 4]

45. *Ṣalāt al-Ghufaylah* written by Saleem Bhimji[4 and 7]

46. *Secrets of the Ḥajj* written by Ayatullah al-Uzma Shaykh Ḥusayn Mazaheri and translated by Saleem Bhimji[2 and 4]

47. Simplified Islamic Laws for Youth and Young Adults according to the edicts of Ayatullah al-Uzma Sayyid ʿAli al-Ḥusayni al-Sistani and translated by Saleem Bhimji[1]

48. Simplified Islamic Laws for Youth and Young Adults according to the edicts of Ayatullah al-Uzma Shaykh Lutfullah Safi Gulpaygani and translated by Saleem Bhimji[5]

49. *Sunan al-Nabī* written by ʿAllamah Sayyid Muḥammad Ḥusayn Taba'taba'i and translated by Tahir Ridha-Jaffer[4]

50. *Tafsir of Sūrahul Jinn* by Ayatullah al-Uzma Shaykh Nasir Makarim Shirazi and translated by Saleem Bhimji[1 and 3]

51. *Taʿqībāt: The Daily Prayers* compiled and translated by Saleem Bhimji and Arifa Hudda[1, 4 and 7]

52. The Firmest Armament: Commentary on Āyatul Kursī [The Verse of the Throne] written by Sayyid Nasrullah Burujerdi and translated by Saleem Bhimji[4]

53. *The Islamic Moral System: A Commentary of Sūrahul Ḥujurāt* written by Ayatulalh Jaʿfar Subhani and translated by Saleem Bhimji[1 and 3]

54. *The Last Luminary and Ways to Delve into the Light* written by Sayyid Muḥammad Ridha Ḥusayni Mutlaq and translated by Saleem Bhimji[4 and 7]

55. The Light of the Family of the Prophet – A Colouring Book with Ḥadīth for Young Muslim Children translated by Saleem Bhimji[1]
56. The Pure Life written by Ayatullah al-Uzma Sayyid Muḥammad Taqi al-Modarresi with translation by Jaffer Ladak and Commentary by Jaffer Ladak and Zainali Panjwani
57. *The Tasbīḥ of Fāṭima al-Zahrā'* written by 'Abbas Azizi and translated by Arifa Hudda and Saleem Bhimji[1]
58. *The Third Testimony: Imam Ali in the Adhan* compiled and translated by Saleem Bhimji
59. The Torch of Perpetual Guidance - A Commentary on Ziyārat al-'Āshūrā' written by 'Abbas Azizi and translated by Saleem Bhimji[4 and 7]
60. *Weapon of the Believer* written by 'Allamah Muḥammad Baqir Majlisi and translated by Saleem Bhimji[4 and 7]
61. *Ziyārah: History, Philosophy and Etiquette* compiled and translated by Saleem Bhimji[4]

To be published, Inshā-Allah (God Willing):

1. *A Year with Prophet Muḥammad* written by Saleem Bhimji, Arifa Hudda and Muhadditha Fatema Saleem
2. *Islamic Marriage and Divorce Processes* compiled by Saleem Bhimji
3. *Khums: The Fiscal Blueprint for Community Self-Sufficiency* written by Saleem Bhimji

4. *People of the Frontiers - Commentary on the Supplication for the People of the Frontiers* by Imam ʿAlī ibn al-Ḥusayn Zayn al-ʿĀbidīn ﷺ written by Shaykh Ḥusayn Anṣāriyān and translated by Saleem Bhimji
5. *Pray As You See Me Pray* according to the edicts of Ayatullah al-Uzma Sayyid ʿAli al-Ḥusayni al-Sistani and translated by Saleem Bhimji1
6. *Sex and Spirituality in Islam* written by Ali Husseinzadeh and translated by Saleem Bhimji
7. *The Ninth Day – The Day of ʿArafah* compiled and translated by Saleem Bhimji and Arifa Hudda
8. *Young Muslims' Daily Devotions - Volumes 1, 2, 3 -* compiled and translated by Saleem Bhimji and Arifa Hudda
9. *Victor Not Victim: Zaynab al-Kubrā* – translated by Saleem Bhimji

...and more to come, Insha-Allah (God Willing)

ABOUT THE ISLAMIC PUBLISHING HOUSE

عَنْ أَبِي عَبْدِ اللّٰهِ عَنْ آبَائِهِ ﷈: قَالَ جَاءَ رَجُلٌ إِلىٰ رَسُولِ اللّٰهِ ﷺ فَقَالَ يَا رَسُولَ اللّٰهِ مَا الْعِلْمُ؟ قَالَ أَلإِنْصَاتُ. قَالَ ثُمَّ مَهْ؟ قَالَ أَلإِسْتِمَاعُ. قَالَ ثُمَّ مَهْ؟ قَالَ أَلْحِفْظُ. قَالَ ثُمَّ مَهْ؟ قَالَ أَلْعَمَلُ بِهِ. قَالَ ثُمَّ مَهْ يَا رَسُولَ اللّٰهِ؟ قَالَ: نَشْرُهُ.

Abū ʿAbdillāh narrates from his ancestors ﷈ who said the following: "A man once came to the Messenger of Allah ﷺ and said, 'O' Messenger of Allah, what is knowledge?' The Prophet replied, **'It is silence.'** The man then asked, 'Then what?' The Prophet said, **'It is listening.'** The man asked, 'Then what?' The Prophet replied, **'Then it is remembering.'** The man asked, 'Then what?' The Prophet said, **'Then it is to practice (according to what one has learned).'** The man then asked, 'Then what O' Messenger of Allah?' The Prophet replied, **'Then it is to disseminate (what one has learned).'**"[44]

Established in early 2001, gaining inspiration from the above quoted statement from Prophet Muḥammad ﷺ, the *Islamic Publishing House* has developed into Canada's premier publisher of high quality Islāmic literature for Muslims of all ages. Our mission is to ensure that the authentic teachings of normative Islām – in all aspects of life – as exemplified by Prophet Muḥammad ﷺ and his immaculate family, the Ahlul Bayt ﷈, are made available for everyone in a clear and easy to understand language.

---

[44] *Al-Kāfī*, vol. 1, pg. 48, trad. 4.

Over the past several years, we have been fortunate to publish **30 full length texts** which have been distributed throughout the world in print; released **7 ePublications;** and authored hundreds of articles - all thanks to the blessings of Allah ﷻ, the grace of the Prophet ﷺ and the Ahlul Bayt ؑ and the continued material support from donors all over the world.

With the ever changing landscape of how and where we consume information, we have embarked upon the creation of what we term, '***Visualations***' in which we fuse together audio, video and the written word to develop a unique educational experience – videos which are uploaded to our YouTube channel and also on the station at Shia TV – garnishing tens of thousands of viewers.

Our publications and video productions are all financially supported by the generous donations of individuals and non-Profit institutions in North America and Europe, for whom we are eternally grateful.

As we continue to produce English publications and unique and original video content, we continually appeal to all of those people who have a passion for the spread of the faith of Islām, as taught by the family of the Prophet ؑ - to assist us in any way possible in promoting the teachings of Islām as taught by Prophet Muḥammad ﷺ and the Ahlul Bayt ؑ.

HOW CAN **YOU** GET INVOLVED?

PROMOTE our content - books, videos, etc... with your contacts on social media and within your local communities in addition to your circle of family and friends.

VOLUNTEER your time and talents to assist us with our print publications or our video content and help us to expand our global reach via social media.

SUPPORT our work by generously donating any money or financial assistance towards content creation and the costs associated with publications, video production and future initiatives.

SUGGEST content which you feel is needed for Muslims to better understand their faith, or to educate non-Believers which is not already available in print or video.

HELP us by making du'a – supplication – to Allah for our guidance and success in our efforts to spread the teachings of Islam to others and educate them.

To support us in any of the ways mentioned above, please contact us at **iph@iph.ca**

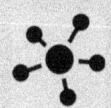

www.ingramcontent.com/pod-product-compliance
Lightning Source LLC
Chambersburg PA
CBHW031655040426
42453CB00006B/316